Always Water

A MEMOIR

EVA H. SAUNDERS

BALBOA.PRESS
A DIVISION OF HAY HOUSE

Balboa Press books may be ordered through booksellers or by contacting:

Balboa Press
A Division of Hay House
1663 Liberty Drive
Bloomington, IN 47403
www.balboapress.com
844-682-1282

Because of the dynamic nature of the Internet, any web addresses or links contained in this book may have changed since publication and may no longer be valid. The views expressed in this work are solely those of the author and do not necessarily reflect the views of the publisher, and the publisher hereby disclaims any responsibility for them.

The author of this book does not dispense medical advice or prescribe the use of any technique as a form of treatment for physical, emotional, or medical problems without the advice of a physician, either directly or indirectly. The intent of the author is only to offer information of a general nature to help you in your quest for emotional and spiritual well-being. In the event you use any of the information in this book for yourself, which is your constitutional right, the author and the publisher assume no responsibility for your actions.

Any people depicted in stock imagery provided by Getty Images are models, and such images are being used for illustrative purposes only.
Certain stock imagery © Getty Images.

Print information available on the last page.

ISBN: 979-8-7652-3678-9 (sc)
ISBN: 979-8-7652-3679-6 (e)

Balboa Press rev. date: 12/06/2022

To my beloved children, Charmaine and Rod, and their children, Max, Joy, Natalie, and Jamie.

I felt compelled to tell them where we come from, the hardships that took place in our lives, and the joys of being able to create a better future for them and their families. It is not always easy to recall the painful past, but it's always educational to learn from it and not repeat it. I devoted my life to overcoming the difficult early years and helping others do the same.

I also dedicate this to my late husband, Emery, the children's father, who spent eight years of his youth in a political prison, five of those in solitary confinement, for supplying information to the West. It left its mark on him emotionally.

Last, but not least, I dedicate this book to Joe Saunders, my second husband, the man who taught me unconditional love; the one who changed my life, and the life of everyone with whom he came in contact, for the better. He was the most nonjudgmental, caring individual I have ever met. Thank you!

The Greatest Influences in my Life:

The Bible – 1940s
Paul Brunton: *A Hermit in the Himalayas* – 1960s
Harvey Jackins: Re-evaluation counseling – 1970s
Werner Erhard: EST training – 1980s
Tony Robbins: Life training – 1990s
Frank Sabatino: Healthy living – 1980s
John Friend: Anusara yoga – 2000s
Paul Brandt: "Don't tell me the sky's the limit when there are footprints on the moon."

Also, my parents, my many wonderful teachers, and my children. I thank you all!

Contents

≈

*I*ntroduction

≈

*A*s the title indicates, water has always been an important part of my life and that of my family. Whenever life was hard, I found myself near water to calm me; it soothed as a balm.

The property where I was born was at the conjunction of two rivers that flowed into the Danube. It was our swimming hole and skating rink. Here we learned to row our boat and nearly drowned a few times.

Mother's home in Vienna was near a tributary of the Danube.

When we found our first home in Chicago it was near Lake Michigan's shores.

The home where I raised my children was in Lake Bluff, also near the lake.

As I moved downtown to be near my business, I always had a lovely lake view.

Finally, when Joe proposed to me, and I realized our new home in Maine was right on the waters of Lake Maranacook, I knew I had found my place!

We purchased a retirement home in Sarasota, Florida, right on the white-sand beaches of Lido Key, where I live out my dream in paradise! I am fortunate to have both sunrise and sunset views, where watching the sunset over the water is a daily pleasure. It is never the same twice!

I also use "water" metaphorically, as water cleanses and washes away all dirt and darkness of the past, and allows the future to be clean and bright, as my life illustrates.

Mother's Family, Englert

〜

Mother's great-grandfather, Joachim Englert, was a diamond cutter and pearl merchant. He married the beautiful Anna Dolezal, and they were known as the "holy family," like the couple in the Bible with the same name who were the Virgin Mary's parents. He traveled far and wide for his stones, and every time he returned home he got her pregnant. Their first was a boy, Agoston (Guszti), followed by six girls: Stefania, Gizella, Valeria, Elizabeth, Clementine, and Ludmilla. The family had their hands full making sure all the girls married well, but Guszti never married. They were spread between Bratislava, Vienna, and Budapest, all part of the Austro-Hungarian Empire.

Valeria, Mother's mom, married Ferdinand von Beck, a very handy auto mechanic and expert who was hired by Guszti to run his automobile shop in Bratislava. The rest is history. They had Mausi (Valerie), and eight years later a son named Ferdinand, who grew up loving anything mechanical and became an engineer.

The family moved to Moson, where grandfather Beck opened the first auto, motorcycle, and bicycle repair shop on the main road between Budapest and Vienna. Not only was he good at his occupation, but he also took up bicycle racing, rowing, swimming, and figure skating because his home was so close to the River Danube. He loved life, wine, his children, and had a great sense of humor. He was a sturdy, athletic, active man, with a bald head and round face, my favorite. I often sat in his lap, and he allowed me to taste some of his red wine, which I am still fond of today.

Father's Family, Molnar

Since Molnar, my grandfather, learned the art of furniture making from a master craftsman, and once he finished, he traveled to see and learn. He took his sisters along to find them a place at the Viennese court, where they could hopefully make a good marriage.

He was of midheight and very strong, muscular with a sense of purpose. He was liked by the ladies, and he married the wealthy Anna Takacs, who provided much land. It was not a very happy union: out of seven children born, six died. Elsa, the oldest daughter, lived to be nineteen; she died of pneumonia just before her wedding. All the other five died before the age of three. Eugene, our father, was the only surviving child out of the seven. Naturally, he was protected and shaded from all peril. Losing so many children left my poor grandmother devastated. She turned to religion for consolation and lost all interest in daily life, for she suffered from severe depression. Eugene earned his diploma in Sopron in furniture design and drafting, which enabled him to continue Grandfather's furniture business. The sign on the storefront became "Vince Molnar and Son Furniture Empire." Grandfather knew Eugene needed a strong business partner in his life if he were to inherit all the wealth Grandfather had accumulated. So he designated Mausi Valerie Beck as Eugene's future wife to assure the survival of the estate. Mausi was raised to be a businesswoman. She was told by grandfather Beck to use her mind and talents properly and not to waste her time on household duties, which could be done by hired help, so she followed his advice.

The wedding took place on December 26, 1938, just as Eugene was about to join the armed forces, taking the family Mercedes with him; it was the beginning of WWII. There was no time to create a beautiful handmade wedding gown, so Mausi purchased a leopard-skin coat and a hat-and-muff set from the large furrier in Gyor, and Eugene wore a gray wool coat lined and collared in red fox. They looked like a couple out of Dr. Zhivago, stunning and unique!

Mausi took control of the business and spent most of her days supervising everything that had arrived or left the store, even though she became pregnant almost immediately. Father was moved to the Russian front in Kiev, where he took a last picture of our beloved Mercedes, and the war began for us personally.

Our Home, Mosonmagyarovar

Once upon a time, long, long ago, there lived a family named Molnar in the town of Movar. It was a merchant family in a typical town setting, right in the middle of a commercial street. The building had a large storefront and big display windows for the furniture and accessories they sold to make a home complete.

The manufacturing took place way in the back of the property, running down to the river in a long shop with machinery and bright lights.

First came the storefront, which was important to show off the merchandise to best advantage. Then came the offices, and finally it all connected to the living quarters of the owner's family. There was plenty of storage for the raw material as well as the finished products. The property had large wooden gates where the trucks and wagons came and went, delivering goods and bringing fresh supplies.

The center court was large so that many wagons could be loaded and unloaded at the same time. Across from the living quarters stood a big two-story building, which acted as storage on the ground floor with apartments above that were leased out to families and provided a steady flow of income. Also on the ground level was the apartment for our gardener, who looked after the orchard of many fruit trees as well as the vegetable gardens and the lovely flower gardens in front of our house. There was a beautiful gazebo where we had our meals in nice weather, located close to the kitchen for easy service. It had two cypress trees on either side and was surrounded by fragrant lilac bushes, a large grassy area for us to play in, and hydrangeas with many blooms.

The property had huge wooden gates, which were always locked at night but were opened first thing in the morning by our porter, who lived in a room under the covered gateway. Next to his quarters was the upholsterer's shop, which had many colorful fabric samples covering the walls. Two bare bulbs hung from the ceiling to provide light for their tasks, since there were no windows and only big double doors to the covered gateway. Two men and a young apprentice worked there for long hours, chatting while they worked.

The inner courtyard housed a blacksmith shop, all black and smoky. The blacksmith always wore an oversized leather apron and gloves and a leather cap tipped to one side, creating a sinister look. Next to him was the big garage, which used to house the fancy family carriages and now sheltered a shining De Dion-Bouton, an early French automobile. The proud mechanic cleaned, shined, and caressed its lacquered surface. The De Dion-Bouton, was followed by a Porsche and later replaced by a Mercedes. The mechanic was also in charge of the delivery truck, which had recently replaced the horse-drawn wagon for faster delivery. This was especially useful for funerals, which were produced within a short timeframe, for coffins were ordered at the time of death and custom-made. They had to be delivered in time for both the wake and the funeral and often had plush lace linings and gold trimmings, according to the means of the surviving family members.

Well-to-do newlyweds usually ordered kitchen cupboards, table and chairs, and a large chipping block. If their space provided, they would get a bedroom set consisting of a bed, nightstand, chest of drawers, and maybe an armoire. Mattresses were often homemade and filled with straw, feather, or horsehair, which was more expensive but lasted a lifetime! Any young woman worth her salt had a mattress and a chest filled with embroidered linen by the time she reached marrying age. If she was very fortunate, she also had some kitchen items: a stove, iron skillets, pots and pans, and the necessary dishes. But this was a rare case.

The courtyard was alive with an orderly hustle-bustle, but as soon as the church bells rang for noon, it all stopped for the awaited lunch break. Peace and quiet settled over the yard, and everyone enjoyed a lovely meal. We had our family, and the office manager Frederick (Frici), Martin the bookkeeper, and sometimes even out-of-town shoppers joined us for this meal, which was usually several courses, the big meal of the day.

We were a happy family, for we could sense the love between Mother and Father. It was just the way they looked at each other and the way they communicated with each other. It was comforting, loving, and warm and made me feel secure.

The End of the Short-Lived Peace

~

I t was a time of worldly pleasures! Theaters were packed, music filled the air, champagne flowed, and everyone lived for the moment, sensing the inevitable just around the corner. People worked hard and played hard, creating ostrich politics.

Our family was no exception. Every weekend was filled with plans. Our house became a center for friends and relatives—Mother at the piano, Dad playing his violin, singing filling the rooms. Some even started to dance. I first learned to dance at these enchanted Sunday evenings with Uncle Nandi, Dad, or some friends. These happy memories lived with me and kept me insulated over the difficult years; they are etched into my heart and soul.

Winters were even more intimate. We gathered around the huge fireplace with its smoldering logs, playing board games, cards, and chess. Tea, coffee, and brandy were served, and good conversation was always going on way into the night.

Our grandmothers, with their knitting and embroideries, occasionally added to the conversation with busy hands quietly working. At dinner, grandpa Beck always allowed us a little red wine to toast everyone: "Egeszsegedre!"—to your health in Hungarian. There were beautiful, tasty meals created by the cook, who had been with us ever since Mother and Dad got married. She had learned her cooking skills at her mom's house.

In nice weather, we kids were perched in the front and back of the adult's bicycles for the long journey to Szigetkoz, the island formed by the Danube. The ride alone was a joy, bumping over the dirt roads, stopping only for a drink from the stream or an emergency stop in the bushes. We rested on large straw piles, where sandwiches were magically produced, along with fruit and drinks, after which we played ball, chased after deer, or played hide and seek. Some collected wild flower bouquets, enjoying the simple pleasures.

Once summer arrived, we kids were packed into the long, narrow rowboats, which the men rowed all the way to the island, pursuing the curving river. The ladies followed by car or a horse-drawn carriage, bringing the picnic, wine and kegs of beer, and music. These were carefree times! Everyone went swimming in the cold river and dried off in the warm sun; then came the food. After eating and drinking, we sat around the glowing coals of the fire listening to stories being told, mostly by Daddy, who was a good storyteller. The taste of early things live on: the smell of wood burning combined with freshly roasted game will always evoke these special moments in my life.

Time raced. The good and the bad happened at such speed it was difficult to follow or believe. Soon all able-bodied men were called into service, the Jewish population was dragged into camps, and children contracted diseases that had no cure. Many injured soldiers came back from hell, maimed and bleeding with body parts missing. Many were blinded and broken physically as well as in spirit. You could hear their cries in the nights, which only the shrieking of the raiding bombs would swallow.

The year was 1944, Mother was expecting her third child, and the happy, carefree days were just a memory. German soldiers were still in charge, using all of our resources without asking. There was fear in the air, and as young as I was, I could sense it. "Did you hear from the front?" was a common question. We did not hear from Father for a long time, and had no clue as to whether he was alive or dead.

The business was focused on coffins and funerals, not much in the way of furniture or interiors. Our faithful Martin, the bookkeeper, who was Jewish and had escaped from Romania, was a fixture in the office. He ran things smoothly, until one day he did not show up. We soon got word that he had been able to get to the West and stay with friends in London. We missed him, along with his dry humor and his very delicate handwriting.

Louise, our governess, tried her best to make us girls believe all would be well, but we could see beyond the words. Her actions and body language told a different story, for she was uneasy. She was a spinster at thirty-five, who always wanted children of her own, and loved and cared for us girls. She came from the country when Edith was born, and lived with us like a family member. She had a room at the end of the house, and had to use the outhouse, but she had her meals with us and spent a great deal more time with us girls than Mother ever did. We were aware of her liking one of the factory foreman, a tall, blond, blue-eyed chap, who liked wine and had a nice voice. We all enjoyed his singing, and we noticed she blushed every time he walked by and always smiled at him, so we started to tease her. It's funny how girls notice these things so young,

Life was good, even while father was away in the army. Our business was in the capable hands of Mother and her right-hand-man, Frici, who had a gift for dealing with people, saying what they wanted to hear, and selling. He was the manager, and ran the business in Father's absence. There was the little midget of a man named Varga, who was the porter and opened and closed the big wooden gates every day. He did not like to bathe, so every now and then, all his belongings were burned and new ones provided to eliminate the bugs in his room. He swept the yards and kept them as clean as possible with his brooms handmade from willow branches.

Grandfather Beck, my favorite adult, was also a big part of the family. He would bounce me on his knees, and I would grab the cap off his baldhead, and take a sip of his wine. Oh, how he loved his granddaughters! He told us stories, and we learned to have high regard for bread and wine, for I could never waste either.

The year was 1944. It was a cold February morning, and the Germans were still the occupiers, when I became very ill with high fever and chills. Our local doctor and friend could not break the fever or even identify the cause. I was only three years of age, and my fever ran as high as 104 degrees Fahrenheit, so Mother was very worried. Our family doctor suggested we contact an army doctor, who might be able to diagnose it, for I was not responding to any medication or remedy. At this point, Mother bravely walked into the German army headquarters, a small garrison, carrying my feverish body and asked if they could take me to their doctor. They put us in an open jeep where I just kept shivering. I was wrapped in Mother's warmest fur coat, the snow began to fall in beautiful, large flakes, and the wind blew the snow in our faces as they rushed us to the larger German camp outside of town. Mother tried to protect me from the snow, but it was a losing battle, it just kept falling and blowing and covering us. The German doctor fully examined me, gave me a shot, and announced I had typhus. Now we had to make the trip back through the heavy snow to the local hospital where we entered total isolation. Mother was with me day and night it seemed. I was put on a liquid diet, and I know Mom was afraid she might lose me. But my body responded to the shot, and the fever broke. I was hungry and asking for food, but was given only some broth and water. To keep occupied, I was drawing all the time. Mother kept bringing colored pencils and paper to keep me busy. I am not sure how long I was in that hospital room, but I do remember the day I was allowed to go home. When we arrived, there was a wonderful fragrance of something sweet and delicious baking in the kitchen. They tucked me into bed, and I fell fast asleep.

When I awoke, the smell was distinctly coming from nearby. I was feeling much better, but still on liquids only. I got out of bed, saw the wonderful dessert cooling on the window sill, and immediately helped myself to a slice, the taste of which I can still recall. Then I took another, and just as I was reaching for a third slice, Louise walked in and found me out. Having been so sick saved me from being punished, and we all hoped it would do me no harm.

The taste and smell of this delicacy lives on, and it's still my favorite dessert—called "Ladies Delight." I am including the recipe so you may try it also!

Ladies Delight recipe
The dough:
1 cup sweet butter
3 1/4 cups flour
pinch of salt
1/2 cup sugar
1 egg yolk
3 1/2 cups sour cream
Cut the butter into the dry ingredients and work all together into a smooth dough; divide in half and refrigerate to chill.
The filling:
3 1/2 pounds cooking apples

1/2 cup dry breadcrumbs

4 tablespoons sugar

1/3 cup chopped walnuts

1 teaspoon cinnamon

2 tablespoons grated lemon rind

The meringue:

3 egg whites

1/2 cup sugar

1/2 teaspoon vanilla

Assembly:

Peel and grate apples; mix with all the filling ingredients except the breadcrumbs. Roll out one of the chilled dough pieces and place in the bottom and sides of a 9 x 13-inch prepared pan. Sprinkle with the breadcrumbs; top with the apple filling. Now roll out the second dough ball into a rectangle to fit on top, then pinch and seal the sides. Carefully, with a fork, prick the top to allow moisture to escape. Brush with egg wash; refrigerate before baking.

Bake at 375 degrees F for 50 minutes or until golden brown.

Now beat egg whites, sugar, and vanilla for the meringue; brush over the pastry and put in a hot oven, 425 degrees F, and bake until it's browned. Cool and enjoy!

Finally young Ferdinand, (Mother's younger brother) was called for military duty. He was sent to the western front, just like his father, grandpa Beck.

The change from German to Russian dominance happened very quickly. We had to escape to the dreaded bomb shelter when the sirens began their shrilling sound, which soon was followed by bomber planes. We were squeezed like sardines into the already prepared blankets, and could hear the crying and grumbling of fellow neighbors all crowded into the small dark dank space, trying to make sense of this senseless situation. Bombs were falling, and we heard large explosions, followed by quiet for a few minutes. Then came the shrilling sound of more eruptions, which burned down factories and army headquarters. By the time it was over, maybe the color of the uniforms had changed, but not much else. Cruelty reigned, men against men, some holding a weapon for the first time and using it on anyone they did not like. The order of things was turned upside down—those educated and capable and running the country were now killed, tortured; those who had no voice and no education were suddenly running things, very poorly.

Nyuszi Is Born, 1945

Under these terrible circumstances, on March 30, 1945 at 10 p.m., while the bombs were falling and we were all hiding out in the shelter, Mother went into labor. Assisted by a midwife, she gave birth to her third daughter, Piroska, so named for having been born so close to Easter Sunday. We had been on our way out of Hungary and escaping into Czechoslovakia, where Mother's Aunt Mila and Fano, her husband, were anxiously waiting our arrival. However, when Mother's labor pains came, it stopped us. We sought shelter in a small village called Halaszi, where Edith and I found room among the already sleeping families lying on straw spread out across the floor for bedding. Father decided to make his way back home and get some food, not realizing the Germans had blown up the bridges over the Danube while fleeing. He had to climb over the wreckage to make his way home and back. He just barely made it, balancing precariously over ruins.

On April 1, 1945, the sirens started up before the sun rose, and we were all rushed into the dreaded shelter for our safety. Mother decided to stay in the bedroom with her tiny infant, trusting in faith and God. Before sunrise on Easter Sunday, the Russians arrived, creating even more fear in the already terrified population. Having been the victors of this war, they lived up to the battlefield traditions of robbing, molesting, raping, and acting like the conquerors they seemed to be, for this was now their bounty. We all feared the worst. Mother, who remained in the bedroom, was attacked by a drunken soldier. As she was screaming and fighting him off, she was saved by an officer. The officer grabbed the offender and tossed him out, and was able to speak to Mother, who was fluent in Slavic languages. This saved her and her baby.

He even assigned a soldier to guard her room to make sure it wouldn't happen again. The moment we laid eyes on our newborn sister, we jointly called out: "Nyuszika" or Easter bunny, and the name stuck—it was her nickname for life.

The first rule of action was that the German language was banned. The German radio stopped broadcasting—no more "Lily Marlene." The German soldiers were replaced by Russians, who seemed far more primitive, grabbing every watch they saw. Some had three or four on each arm. The uniforms changed, but the terror remained. The Russians were also very fond of horses, and took every one they could find from the terrified farmers at gunpoint. Little Nyuszi grew under these circumstances, seeking nourishment and warmth from Mother's breast but, unfortunately, not for long.

Life for our family became unbearable. We were now considered "enemies of the people" since we had accumulated wealth. Suddenly it was all taken from us, distributed among those who had none and did not know what to do with it. Before long, Russian tanks rumbled through town, and we were picked up, banished from our own home.

Deportation

—

When WWII ended, all the citizens with German last names were gathered up and deported. Since Mother's maiden name was Beck, which made her a suspect even though she had been a Hungarian citizen with no political affiliation, she was one of the many innocents who was picked on. It was late one evening when men in dark suits came banging on the door, demanding that Mother and the three girls go with them. Mother had the infant, Nyuszi, in her arms, and we were hanging on to her skirts as we were pushed onto the waiting truck, where many others had already been collected.

We were driven to the railroad station, where all of us were herded into an animal transport wagon with some straw spread on the floor, our bodies packed tight. Mother told us not to let go of each other, so Edith and I hung on fiercely, determined not to get separated no matter what. Mother was nursing little baby Nyuszi and keeping her covered and protected. It was cold, and we were hungry and tired and shivering, unprepared for this unexpected turn of events. We needed to use the bathroom, but there was none. Poor Mother had no food or drink, and the baby just kept nursing while the train kept moving all night. The rumor spread that we were heading for Siberia and the Gulag (forced labor camps). One old man took pity on us, took off his jacket, and covered us girls with it. In the morning the engine stopped.

We were standing still for a long time before we realized they were taking the engine away. We just remained on the tracks without the engine.

Someone yelled, "Let's break out of this prison," and they started tugging on the sliding panels of the wagon for some much needed fresh air. Edith and I scrambled out and walked for a long time until we found a dilapidated farmhouse where a dog barked angrily. We told the farmer woman what had happened and that we needed some food and milk for Mother. She gave us some water from the well and some bread and pickles, but she said that was all she had. Of course we were delighted to be taking something back to Mother and the nice man who had given us his jacket. But once we got back, we found the man was lying still. The poor creature was dead.

Fortunately, our governess Louise and the manager Frederick found out where we had been taken and came with plenty of food and milk for Mother. They collected the three of us girls and took us home. But Mother was detained; she was not allowed to leave the train. She had to stay, and her nightmare began. She was transported to the much-feared political prison "Andrassy-ut 60," which is now the "Museum of Horrors," in Budapest. Here she was tortured and raped and mistreated, things she never wanted to talk about later. It would be ten years before we would see her again in 1956.

Life was never the same without Mother. Our father was alone with the three little girls and the governess was in charge of us. We were no longer the loving family that Mother's presence had kept so alive and happy.

Hungary had been devastated three times: First by the treaty in Trianon after WWI, when it was ripped apart by politicians; then came Yalta, with further divisions; and finally Stalin's reign of terror and murder following WWII, which took place within the now shrunken borders of what remained of Hungary. During and after the war, thousands escaped to the West to find new opportunities before the Iron Curtain came down. Hungarians were scattered across the globe, their hearts bursting with hope-filled dreams. There are few countries in the world that have not received some Hungarian refugees; they are hardworking, well-educated, peace-loving individualists, generally welcomed in most places.

Communism Reigned

~

*I*n 1949, the Communist Party won the election overwhelmingly. They imported Stalin-educated "overseers" from the Soviet Union (CCCP) for all important positions in the now communist countries of the Eastern Bloc. Our new leaders were well versed in the Stalinist, Leninist, and Marxist dogmas, which were introduced into our educational systems throughout the Eastern Bloc countries. It meant physical and mental torture and the destruction of the middle class, as well as the dissolution of the gentry, the landowners, and the wealthy. All this was done step by step. Everything was taken from those who had learned to manage things, and given to those who had never had anything and felt no appreciation or respect for it. Unfortunately, the beautifully sounding theories of communism never worked in practice. That is the reason it all failed, ending with "the collapse of the wall" on November 9, 1989.

The leaders from Moscow were dictators, exerting total control without any responsibility to anyone. We lived in fear! The prisons were filled to capacity, and spies would give up their own mothers out of self-preservation. You could not trust anyone or say even a word against the system. Cardinal Mindszenty, the celebrated head of the Catholic Church, was now among the accused and was found guilty. Everyone at home was secretly listening behind closed doors to Radio Free Europe's broadcast of his trials. He became a symbol of strength, willing to stand up to his accusers. He was the best known of the many brave heroes who chose torture and prison and horrible deaths over appeasing the dictator's whims.

People disappeared daily, being picked up off the street or never returning home from work. There were false accusations made against anyone who was not willing to work with the party. Those unwilling often ended up as food for the fish in the Danube. The Rakosi slogan was "Whoever is not with us is against us!" This meant if you did not turn red, it could cost you your life. Even fashion was a sign of decadence. So was religion, classical music, and foreign languages. You had to be an atheist who believed only in Stalin.

Trials were a joke. Many people were falsely accused, sentenced to death, and executed that very day without a chance to defend themselves. The newspapers started writing in symbols, to make sure people understood they were censored. All children of school age were "Pioneers," and not by choice. You had to wear the stupid red scarf to indicate your membership.

Notre Dame de Sion

~

Suddenly, it was the fall of 1946, the start of a school year. I was only five, but Edith had turned six, and was sent away to boarding school in Budapest. It was very difficult for me. We were so close and did everything together; the days seemed long without my playmate and best friend. I could hardly wait for the year to end to be old enough to join her at Notre Dame de Sion, the French boarding school operated by nuns from France. Everyone talked about it as if one was going to heaven, but soon enough I found out what it really was like.

The day finally arrived, in September 1947, when we two sisters took the train together for the journey to the big city and on to the Sion on Eagle Mountain.

Parts of this stately castle on top of the mountain were still bombed out. The chapel lay in ruin, and much of the gardens were overgrown with weeds. There were even some unexploded bombs lying around. We had to speak French, for the only classes taught in Hungarian were math and literature. Edith had nothing but good memories. She loved the school and the nuns, and was practicing her French on anyone willing to engage. She told me stories about the friends she made and the homes she was invited to, and was bursting with enthusiasm for the upcoming year. She even talked about her love of some nuns, especially Mother Superior, whom she adored. They awaited us at the station since they knew we would be coming with a heavy load of food from the country, where supplies were plentiful. The city still suffered from the effects of war, with bombed out storefronts and food shortages. We arrived with big sacks of beans, flour, sugar, and lard, all important to feed the many privileged girls. We even brought some homemade soaps, which were not at all available in the city, as well as our own linens.

My first morning, we were awakened in the dark at five in the morning, and had to hurry with our washing and dressing so as to be ready for mass by six and breakfast at seven. I wanted to stay under the warm covers, but had to rush and wait in line to use the only working sink and toilet. No one could miss mass without special permission. So, with sleepy eyes and an oversized uniform, which was cold and heavy, I settled into the bench, ready for a little more snoozing. My classmates next to me started cruelly poking me to stay awake!

After mass we lined up for what seemed to be the worst breakfast of my life: imitation coffee made from roasted barley, served with powdered milk that smelled. This was the only milk available in the city since the war, and I could not swallow it, coming from a home where we had our own cow and plenty of fresh milk for hot cocoa. I was informed about the rules: you had to eat everything you were served no matter what! I said I simply could not swallow this trash, so I was locked up in the gym with the food until I ate it. They wanted to make a point, but being as stubborn as I was, there was no way I would give in. A whole day went by. I was suffering from hunger pains but still would not touch that vile coffee. One of the kinder nuns took pity on me and came to offer me some stale bread, disposing of the bad coffee with the promise I would drink it the next morning without the powdered milk. It was still horrible, but at least it did not smell bad.

Edith was loved, excelled in academics, and received the much coveted "cordon," which she wore for all to see as a sign of being an outstanding student. I was loved for my comic mimicry, clowning and making everyone laugh when even talking was not allowed. However, I was punished often for keeping everyone hysterical while eating. Fortunately, Mother Superior liked me and even had a cute nickname for me. Sometimes she lifted a harsh punishment I had been dealt, such as being locked up in the gym overnight for not eating a meal.

It was these saintly nuns who held the building together with prayer and hard work, instilling the highest form of etiquette while providing a fine education to their charges under difficult circumstances. Rules were strict, and we all had to pitch in and do our share of the work. The war may have ended, but it's destruction had to be dealt with by everyone. The roads were beyond repair. Everywhere you looked, there were bullet holes, even on the tall brick walls surrounding the school. The plumbing was still unrepaired, so daily cleansing was challenging. Nuns carried buckets of water from the few faucets that worked, and heated the water on the stove. We each received a bowl to wash in. Once a week, we had a chance to take a real tub bath in the only working bathroom, where we had to wear a long cotton gown for bathing. Nudity was not allowed, and the nuns scrubbed our backs through the garment. There were around two hundred "privileged girls" there at any time, mostly daughters of diplomats or visiting dignitaries, and nearly all of them left for holidays. The few of us who stayed were given special privileges.

My struggle was with the awful food and the once-a-month full-water fast. Our uniforms were navy wool, pleaded skirts that buttoned onto long-sleeved navy blouses with little white collars, which were removed and washed often. In warm weather, our blouses would change to short-sleeved light blue cotton ones. The gym attire was a one-piece navy linen suit.

Mass was said in Latin as were the songs we had to memorize. The nuns were always distant and cold, with no physical contact of any kind toward us except slapping our fingertips with the wooden rulers. Once a month, we were allowed to leave for the weekend. I looked forward to these excursions so much; I was either invited by a kind family or was visiting Uncle Nandi and his family. It was a joy to have a decent meal and be able to sleep in!

There were many strict rules, and some of the mean nuns continued enforcing them during the school year. To me, they appeared harsh; to Edith, they were just being natural. However, once school was out, a handful of us girls stayed on for the summer holiday, and the nuns loosened up on the rules. They tied up their long skirts and ran and played with us. We could climb trees, pick fruit and wild flowers from the gardens, and even play ball. The nuns enjoyed us and were very sympathetic to the fact that we had no home to go to because of various circumstances. Edith and I sometimes got to visit Uncle Nandi and his young family. They lived just outside of the city in the Buda Hills, where we spent many happy weekends with our cousin Cornelia, who we called Nelly.

My Accident

≈

On one of the winter weekends, when Father was visiting, and all of us were staying at Uncle Nandi's villa, we awoke early on Sunday morning. Everyone was enjoying breakfast. I was excited to show Father my sledding skills, so I quietly got dressed, put on my heavy boots, and got the sled out to start practicing. I did not realize the ground was covered with a sheet of ice, and I would have no control over the sled. As I slid down the steep slope, I lost control and headed right into a lamppost located just a few doors down from Uncle's house. My face was completely smashed, and I lost consciousness. A neighbor saw me and called for help, rousing the family. I was carefully lifted into the nearest house, and a doctor was called, but there was no way for him to get up there because of the icy surface. It took a long time, but when the doctor finally arrived, he told Dad that I might not recover from this injury. He said it might be for the best, as I would never be the same.

As this was happening, I had an out of body experience. I was somehow hovering over my injured body lying on the bed, seeing my father so sad and defeated, and hearing what the doctor said. I wanted to scream, but no sound came. I wanted them to know I was fine. Not to worry. I do not know how long I remained in this state, but one morning I woke up and called out, "I am hungry," to everyone's surprise. They had all thought I would never be able to speak again. There was a big celebration, and I was back in school in no time. A week later, Edith had a serious accident, losing her fingernail on the right thumb at the pump. Poor Father had to deal with a lot in those days, without a wife, bearing all the stress by himself.

It was this summer of 1948 when, on a hot night, we saw bright flames engulf a large structure in the middle of the dark city. We soon found out that the beautiful St. Steven's Cathedral was burning! This historic church, which was filled with treasures by famous artists and royal burial vaults in marble and bronze; it was all in flames, the beginning of the end.

Our school was shut. Some of the nuns were jailed and others put on the train for France. The few of us girls who were left were also put on the train for home. It was the end of this famous institution in Hungary. Eventually, the building became a teacher's college, with Russian and Marxist teaching.

We arrived back in our hometown of Mosonmagyarovar, and it was a shock! With Mother gone, it did not feel like home. Nothing was ever the same after that, especially once "she" entered our lives.

Meeting the Devious Stepmother, 1948

≈

On a beautiful sunny afternoon in 1948, Father told us he had a surprise planned. We dressed in our Sunday best and were excited to leave, but were surprised when our father took an unusual route. We biked over to an out-of-the-way house behind the big mansion of the Graf family, whom we heard had escaped to the West some time earlier. Our washing lady lived in the servant quarters of this mansion, and she came once a week to hand-wash all our laundry in big wooden tubs. We loved her, for she had six children, always smiled, and sang beautiful love songs, which we learned from her. She told us stories of life in the big house, the parties, the hunts and balls, and we were transported to another place and time. She was a tiny woman with overworked hands and a lovely spirit, which was very attractive to us. But we had not been taken to see her. We went to a small house behind the mansion but still on the same property, and Father sprung the surprise.

First he introduced us to his new woman, Clara, who was stunning and exotic, with flaming red shoulder-length hair and a form-fitting blue dress that accentuated all her curves. Father was obviously taken by Clara. She tried to interest us in some sweets and introduce us to her mother, who seemed much warmer and had a sweet smile. I was seven, Edith was eight, and Nyuszi was three, and we instantly disliked Clara and wanted nothing to do with either her or her mother. We rode our bikes on the path, walked around the garden, picked some fruit off the trees, and were ready to go. Father kept trying to delay our departure, but when he finally realized how miserable we girls were, he allowed us to leave. We tried to reason with him all the way home, saying that we already had a mother and he a wife, but he said they were separated by the Iron Curtain and could not be together. We begged him not to marry Clara, we hated her, we could take care of him and each other, did not need her! He explained that she would be a good mentor for us. She had been well educated abroad, and had a vast knowledge that she could pass on to us: languages and etiquette, all things we needed to learn from a woman. She lived with her aging mother who was epileptic, and who had managed the estate for the Graf's when they were living there. Since they had left the country, she no longer had her income, and our father would have to help them. We complained bitterly to Louise, our governess, who was also very upset to hear the news. She had a crush on Father, and I am sure was hoping for a union with him under the circumstances. She was hurt and jealous. Things got much worse fast.

There was a civil ceremony in June. None of us girls were present, and Clara and her mom moved in with us, upsetting our life, removing some of our furniture to make room for theirs. And our Louise was fired after all those years with us! We were all miserable. Clara kept trying to get Nyuszi, the youngest, to be her pet. The poor child was so hungry for a little attention and motherly love, she was easily manipulated into a favored role. She was adorable, with dark curls and long lashes, almond-shaped eyes, and a very fair complexion. She looked like a living doll.

We Lose Everything, Fall of 1949

~

October 1949. After a brief honeymoon, the AVO guys (the feared secret police), who said they "represented the people," came one morning to the store that was my father's business and told him he had one hour to gather his personal belongings. They were taking over in the name of the state. So Father went to open the safe, where we kept all our valuables and cash, but they said that was not personal and would not let him touch anything. In a matter of hours, we went from being "the enviable rich" to being paupers. Word spread. Before we knew it, they came to our home and gave us a choice of four rooms out of our large comfortable home. Wisely, Father selected the hallway with the inside toilet and the bathroom. We had to give up our kitchen with running water, which was at the far end of the house. We also lost our bedrooms, and now had to sleep in the new kitchen, which used to be our library. Edith and I shared an old iron folding bed. We had to set it up at night and fold it every morning to make room for cooking and eating. Everything that was done in this house took place in this room. There was no privacy for us, so we slept exhausted every night, and dressed in the only room where all activity happened. We now had to carry buckets of water from the well to this "kitchen" for all our needs: cooking, washing dishes, and the like. In a mockery of justice, the factory was given to the most inept apprentice—a card carrying communist and a drunk. He was now in charge! The rest of the house was divided up between two other "well deserving families."

Life became hell overnight. All the help had been let go. Clara took ill after the news. She simply lay down, telling us girls that from now on we would have to do all the work. We were now poor and needed to learn to make our way in the world. She was not fit for work, having never learned to do it, so we would have to.

Father tried to get employment, but soon found that no one would hire him, for he was considered "an enemy of the people." We had no income—the money we had saved was taken from us along with everything else—and the future looked bleak.

At the age of nine, Edith took charge of the household. With the help of grandma Elizabeth, Clara's mother, they handled shopping, cooking, cleaning, and gave me chores I had to complete. We were able to keep our small animals: chickens, ducks, geese, guinea hens, and a pig. Our cow and horses were given to a farmer who offered us all the milk we needed, we just had to go there daily to get it. This was to be my job. No matter what the weather, I had to ride my bike forty minutes each way to get our milk, which provided the family with butter and cheese as well.

Edith and I now had to wake up at five every morning to take care of the morning chores, fold our collapsible bed, put the bedding away, dress, feed the animals and clean their cages, wash up, and walk the mile to the public girls school. We hated this newcomer, Clara, with her painted nails and bright red hair lying around reading her novels and acting like a queen bee!

Father was devastated and angry most of the time, understandably. He did what he could by going to the woods and collecting firewood, and we also helped him after school. With all the chores I had to do, there was little time to feel sorry for myself. I just kept going until all was done. Then I dropped, exhausted, into the tiny iron bed where Edith and I both slept. Lights went out early, so homework and reading were done under the covers at night by candlelight. It is a wonder we did not go up in flames! One of us would hold the candle, while the other would read or write. Amazingly, we were able to keep relatively good grades, but our previous education helped.

Clara could tell we all still loved each other, because Father was so caring toward us, so she wickedly set out to separate us. The accusations began. At first things disappeared, and we were accused of stealing them, so of course Father would have to beat us. She cheered him on, told him to use his belt, not his hands, and sometimes she even gave him a bamboo stick to use to beat us. She claimed we were spoiled brats and needed severe punishment. Soon the accusations escalated to sexual misbehavior, which we did not even understand. Clara accused Edith and I of having lesbian relations and of trying to spoil our little sister as well. It was all her imagination, since we had no idea what she was talking about, but the beatings continued in order to get us give up our "unnatural actions" and stay away from little Nyuszi. Then we were tied and chained to the bed, and could no longer even do our homework at night since we were unable to use our hands.

We never had any money. Clara sent us to the neighbors to borrow some, which she never returned, but she needed cash to buy wine, of which she was very, very fond. Clara also liked her cats. She had several, always lying around with her on the couch or in bed, and she fed them like humans.

At this point, Edith signed up to work at the local agricultural academy, and the work required skipping school for weeks at a time. However, it did bring income, which Clara took, always sending notes to school saying Edith was ill. Soon summer vacation came, and I also started working in the academy six days a week and getting paid. With the two of us working full-time, it covered the household expenses. Even Father was able to secure a job in a factory. It was far away, and he needed to use the only bicycle we had to commute, so we girls had to walk.

She now decided to visit our school to alert the principle of our lesbian activities. To our total humiliation, we were called in by the local pediatrician and examined and lectured about things we had no clue about. The embarrassment was unbearable, and many more beatings followed. Some days, my bottom was so sore, that I just hid out in the woodshed and cried hysterically, not so much from the physical pain, but from the emotional agony. And poor grandma Elizabeth! Her daughter could hardly tolerate her being in the house. The old lady worked from morning till night in spite of her advanced age and her epilepsy.

Clara again accelerated our situation. She demanded mortifying examinations at school, and required a suitable student to supervise our walk to and from school, for which she was willing to pay from the money we earned. It infuriated us, but what could we do?

Now we began to plot her killing. She was asthmatic and required medication, which Edith had to administer every morning and evening, so we thought perhaps an overdose. It may have worked, but we did not know how much would be fatal, or how effective it would be, so we decided we needed poison. However, after acquiring it, we just did not have the nerve to go through with it. We had a very strong belief in the religious training we had received, and we just could *not* do it, even though it could make our lives better, including grandma Elizabeth's.

We also discovered that Clara was actually selling the items she accused us of selling! Things like Father's custom shirts, shoes, gloves, and even our fur coats from school, which Mother had brought us. We were running around in the cold without proper coats, no gloves or warm boots. Our hands and feet were frozen many times and painfully swollen, which we tried to hide in any social situation. Clara played the poor sick woman who was willing to give up her life to raise these three "abandoned brats," spoiled and misguided by their governess, who—according to her—had indoctrinated us into being lesbians.

Religion was a stronghold in our lives. We were the youngest members of the church choir, and often enjoyed the pleasure of singing in a peaceful environment. Unfortunately, there was no one we could turn to—Clara made sure of that! She had gotten the school and the principal on her side, and made us look evil so no one would listen to us. We often considered suicide, but again, it was against all Catholic teachings. We lived by these rules and believed this was our cross we had to bear.

Then Father befriended someone at work who soon started visiting the house. After becoming friendly with Clara, he invited us girls to his home in Gyor, the next large city, for a little vacation. We felt he was someone Father's age; someone who might be sympathetic to our situation. Just maybe we could trust him and tell him all our grievances. We packed a few belongings, toothbrushes and change of underwear and a nighty, tied them up in a scarf, and were ready to go. The trip was exciting. We had escaped from Clara briefly and might even be able to sleep late! Of course, Nyuszi was not allowed to go anywhere without Clara, so it was just Edith and I.

The man showed us around his house and garden, and there was a flow of people in and out. After a busy afternoon exploring our new surroundings and having a light dinner, we retired and found that the sleeping arrangement was that he was sleeping with us in the same bed, between the two of us. We thought nothing of it, and went to sleep. At one point in the night, Edith screamed and jumped out of bed. He then turned to me and proceeded to molest me. Edith and I had no idea of sex or even the mechanism of how it worked. He frightened us, and it was reason enough not to trust that dreadful man, and just hurry back home to our miserable life with Clara. There was no escape for us, it seemed, and no one we could talk to.

Annual Pig Slaughter

~

Meat was only used to flavor our mostly vegetable diet. However, we always had a pig, which was fattened up on leftovers and scraps over the year and killed after the first big frost of winter. It provided the necessary lard for cooking for the whole year. Dozens of sausages were made, which then were smoked with the ham and bacon for safekeeping. The butcher came early on the designated morning, which we were anticipating, and the pig was killed very quickly with just one hit to the heart by the experienced slaughterer. There was an open fire of straw, where the skin was seared just enough to burn off all the hairs; then the pig was hosed down and cut open to start the processing and preparing of every usable part of the animal. Of course, the blood was saved and turned into blood sausage with hot paprika, chopped onions, hot peppers, and some rice, then forced into casings made from the intestines, which had been boiled clean. The parts that were not usable for anything else were cooked, chopped, and added to the headcheese. The bacon and ham were treasured, and were smoked with all the sausages; there was enough to last for the year! The best part of this day was when the warm boiled flesh was served on big slices of crusty rye bread with freshly grated horseradish, accompanied by some red wine—a feast! There were many friends and neighbors who came to help with all the preparation, and this was the reward.

The tail, ears, snout, and feet became a specialty for New Year's Eve. They were always served in aspic with freshly grated horseradish after being cooked in a wonderful root-vegetable broth, chilled and served cold. The skin of the pig was peeled off and put into the big copper bowl over hot coals, allowing all the fat to liquefy. The crisp bits of skin became cracklings, and were used to flavor pasta, biscuits, and vegetable dishes.

The making of kolbasz, the best Hungarian sausage, was a well-guarded secret recipe of each household. Ours was heavy with garlic, paprika, salt, and just enough spice to give it a kick. It was the choicest of the meat, delicious.

When a chicken was killed, its blood would provide one meal. The large chicken would then be baked to provide another meal. Finally the neck, wings, and giblets would make a delicious soup for yet another meal, with lots of vegetables and dumplings. Egg-laying chickens were rarely killed, for the eggs were valuable for cooking, baking, and meals, and if we had an overabundance of them, they could be sold or traded.

Money was always in short supply, so trading eggs for other needed items came in handy. However, this was the time when Clara began drinking in earnest, mixing her drug dependency with a dose of alcohol, and that cost money.

Finally, when Edith was in fourth grade and I in third, we were able to sign on for the harvesting crew at the local collective farm, which was now state owned. It was probably the hardest of all agricultural jobs, for it was pure manual labor. A man with a large sickle cut the dry wheat, and a young woman kept pace with him, grabbing all the falling wheat in her little catcher. She walked along as fast as he cut, catching the long stems and collecting them all at the end of the row, where they were picked up and added to the machine that separated the stems from the seeds. It was hard, backbreaking work. We learned very early on that the hardest part was when our bare feet stepped on the hard straw that remained after the cutting. It was sharp and tore into the skin, and you bled for a few days until you developed calluses on the soles of your feet; then they would not bleed any longer. I cried a few nights, washing all the dirt out of the open sores, but after they healed, they would toughen. The farm paid us in flour, enough for the whole year's needs.

Bread was an important part of our diet, and making it once a week was a big undertaking. It started the evening before, when we prepared all the ingredients. Usually our bread contained mashed potatoes for more nutrients. We prepared the yeast with warm milk, sugar, and flour to rise overnight; then, the next morning, we got up extra early to start kneading and working the dough until it formed little bubbles. Next we needed to place it in a warm corner, away from any draft, cover it, and wait until it doubled in bulk. Finally, it was kneaded again and shaped into a very large loaf, which we now had to transfer to the nearest bakery, which had the huge ovens. Here they baked it, and we had to pick it up after school. We used a little wagon with four wheels for this, or a sled in winter months. The bread weighed thirty-five to forty pounds, and lasted us the whole week. Very often our lunch was simply a slice of thick crusty bread with lard and paprika and salt.

During harvest we did not go to school; instead we worked the fields, and Clara told the principal we were sick. This happened more frequently as we got older and were able to work longer hours. Edith was very resourceful, making deals, so we took on acres of cornfields to pick, as well as sugar beets, which was backbreaking work, pulling the large beets by hand into baskets. Fortunately, our friends from the academy came to help, and we were able to clear large fields and earn a lot by having extra helping hands. These were seasonal jobs and paid well for young inexperienced girls, so we did just fine.

Occasionally, we were invited by old family friends to tea or some social get-togethers. Here we met boys and girls, learned to embroider, knit, and crochet, and just enjoyed being with friends our age. Unfortunately, our very frozen and swollen red hands were always an embarrassment. We even tried wearing gloves, when we found a pair, to hide them. We even danced sometimes, with someone playing the piano, and that was always enjoyable. These were rare occasions, and memorable.

Trip to Bratislava, Summer of 1956

≈

The most outstanding event was a trip to visit relatives in Bratislava, Czechoslovakia. It was summer, and we had received an invitation from Mother's Aunt Elisa and her husband Uncle Victor to come for a visit. We immediately applied for a visitor's visa, which we were told was very hard to acquire. We patiently went daily to city hall to check on the progress, and after persisting for weeks, we finally received the much coveted visa.

Edith and I excitedly packed a few belongings; we set the date, and wrote to Aunt Elisa when we expected to arrive. The bus trip was full of excitement. We were not only meeting relatives for the first time, we were going to a new city in a different country with a different language. We were thrilled!

Once we arrived in this fairly large city, however, we asked for directions to the address we had, which turned out to be outdated. The whole block had been demolished to make room for a new road. Now here we were, lost, not knowing how we could find our aunt and uncle. We walked, asked, knocked on doors, checked in stores, and finally, met an elderly woman who knew the family. (Their name was originally Doppler, but after the country was renamed Czechoslovakia, the name became Dopplerova, which was more Slavic). The elderly woman was able to give us directions to their house.

It was after dark when we finally arrived—tired, cold, and hungry—to a loving welcome. We talked for hours, and found out that Aunt Mila from Vienna and her sister from New York would be arriving the next day and staying at the elegant Divan Hotel. We had brought our only nice dresses, of navy wool with small white collars, and little sandals with white socks. We felt under dressed, so Aunt Elisa opened her closet and said we could pick any pair of high heels we liked that fit, and even provided nylons, which we had never worn before. We tried on one after the other, feeling like Cinderella, and happily picked the choicest heels. For the first time, we were being treated with respect, like adults. I could barely sleep from the excitement. After a scrumptious breakfast, a lot more questions were asked, and we were finally able to tell the story of our very abusive lifestyle with Clara. The humiliations we had suffered at last fell upon sympathetic ears.

Finally, the much-awaited evening arrived. It was the highlight of our life, arriving at this elegant hotel with the two aunts anticipating our arrival. We met them in the overly bright crystal room, the three lady sisters, Uncle Victor, and the two of us. With cocktails in hand, they asked many questions, again treating us like adults—with respect. Aunt Erna, who had left Vienna for New York after she had lost her musician husband, was wearing the most colorful clothes, dripping in jewelry, and sporting a wide brimmed hat. To us she appeared as "Auntie Mame."

She drove a very fancy convertible, which we rode in all over the city; we were the envy of all who saw us. A new world opened up in front of our eyes. We found out from Aunt Mila that Mother had written letters weekly to us, which Clara would never let us see. The five days we spent in Bratislava were life altering for me! I swore to become "Auntie Mame" myself and to live in the "city that never sleeps." I would have a beautiful car, and be surrounded by sparkling crystals and chandeliers just like those in the hotel we had visited.

It was just weeks later that the revolution would come and our existence would change drastically. I was on the way to accomplishing my dreams.

Once Edith graduated from eight-grade, she was allowed to go to high school because of her good grades (and the principal felt sorry for us). Edith loved school and really deserved to go on to higher education, which is what she'd always wanted. The following year, when my turn came, I was not allowed to attend high school. I was told, in the fall, I had to become an apprentice in the flour mill. This did not thrill me, but there was no choice.

We both worked hard over the summer at the collective farm, and when fall came, I was given a pair of overalls and a scarf to cover my hair and was sent to the nearby flour mill to begin training. Starting out, I was the only girl among several boys. I was terribly shy and uncomfortable in my silly attire, but soon learned that the boys were equally afraid of me, so we became friends. I even started smoking with them, and they showed me how to climb out on the roof, where we could not be seen. We would smoke these very strong, unfiltered Russian cigarettes, which made me cough and cry, but I stuck with it to remain friendly. For lunch, we had tickets to dine at the nearby Black Eagle restaurant, which was a real treat. We could order anything off the lunch menu and so eat some good food. Outside of the food and my new friends, I hated every minute of my new life, and had a vision of being rescued soon. I even told tales to my new friends—of going far away to a land where "all the work was done by machines." No more work for me! I was going to drive one of those fancy cars and have a machine for everything, even washing clothes and the dishes.

My dreams eventually were realized, for so much of it did come true. As soon as we began to hear of the uprising in Budapest, I knew this was my escape from all my misery. The revolution began in October 1956, led by the youth and factory workers, rising together against complete oppression.

Revolution, October of 1956

〜

On the eve of October 26th, we received the news from Radio Free Europe that large numbers of youth, mostly from the universities and the nearby factories, were gathered in front of Parliament Square. Some of the people felt trouble brewing and immediately headed for the border to escape to the West. We heard from eyewitnesses that thousands were gathered to force the Russian troops to leave. They had created a twenty-two-point demand, which they delivered to the leaders of the parliament and the radio station.

Back home, we headed toward the agricultural academy, which was built on Roman ruins with thick stonewalls, surrounded by a mote. It was connected to the local experimental laboratories, where many major trials had taken place conducted by world-famous professors, and where we had both worked during summer vacations since the age of eight.

As soon as we met up with our friends, we started a sympathy gathering. The numbers swelled as we marched toward city hall; people from all walks of life joined in. Signs were created, flags were produced, and the hated communist symbol of hammer and sickle was removed, restoring our original flag of Hungary.

The mood was exciting, and we anticipated that at least some of the twenty-two points would be met and some freedom restored to our life. It was a peaceful gathering. No one had any weapons or was in any way endangering anyone. We simply wanted to be listened to and be heard.

Tragically, as soon as one group headed toward the AVO headquarters, gunshots rang out. Suddenly, people were dropping to the ground to escape being hit.

We were in another group heading to the radio station, but upon hearing the shooting, we all started running toward the noise, and it was total chaos! There were screams, the moaning of the injured, and blood flowing in streams. We were asked to get help from the hospital. Some people were picking up the injured and carrying them to the hospital grounds. Others, who were more experienced, started applying first aid. It was terrible. We were stepping over bodies, identifying the dead, and looking for signs of life among the nonmoving, who were presumed dead. It was totally unexpected and lethal; hundreds were killed and at least as many injured. We were all terrified.

Women arrived carrying white sheets and covering the dead, among them our friends, classmates, and neighbors. Life sped up like never before; there was no time to lose. It was a matter of life or death, and we helped in any way we could: wiping blood from the wounded, applying cloths to stop bleeding, bringing water to the injured, and showing our love. Even children were not spared—several lay among the dead, still clinging to their parents or older siblings. This was just a very small sampling of happenings in the capital, where the dead numbered thousands, and even more were injured. Since all of the armed forces had joined in the revolution, young soldiers now had weapons, and in some cases, even tanks and homemade explosives. Now possessing weapons, the angry crowd started to make their way to the Freedom Square, where the demands were read again. The mob surged toward the jails, where all the political prisoners were locked up, hoping to free them. Radio Free Europe's broadcast kept promising that the USA was on the way to intercede on the side of freedom. It encouraged the fighters to keep going. Help was on the way!

A distant cousin, who lived in Budapest, passed by on his way to Vienna where he was hoping to get medical supplies, which were badly needed. He promised he would stop back on his return to the capital after accomplishing his mission. He told us that all the military as well as the local police sided with the revolution against the occupying Russians. Everyone had had enough of the occupation, and now, with weapons, there was some hope of winning.

When people saw the slaughter of innocents, they turned angry. Now even the police and firemen, as well as most citizens, joined in the fight. They used anything as a weapon while making their demands for a free press, free speech, and no more Russian occupation!

We received news this was happening in all parts of Hungary. People were fed up, and this was their chance to express their anger and frustration. The Radio Free Europe broadcast was very encouraging. It looked possible, against all odds, that if help arrived in time, we could win. However, even though it appeared that the revolutionaries were winning, on the morning of November 4th (Edith's sixteenth birthday), we woke to the sound of tanks rumbling down the main roads, with Russian flags flying. We knew it was all over—the enemy had won. As the tanks rattled through our streets, their drivers asked, "where is the Suez Canal?"

Help never arrived. The Suez Crisis seemed far more important to politicians than a little, insignificant country's cry for help for its freedom. Even the British shut their eyes to our desperate pleas. All of our allies deserted us, and the Russian reinforcement marched in with heavy artillery and crushed the revolt.

"a quote from James a Michener, in his book HE BRIDGE AT ANDAU which is his account of the 1956 Revolution he writes:

"In this book I propose to tell The story of a terror so complete as to be deadening to the senses. I shall have to relate the details of a planned bestiality that is revolting to the human mind, but I do so in order to remind myself and free men everywhere that there is no hope for any nation or group that allows itself to be swept into the orbit of international communism. There can be only one outcome: terror and the loss of every freedom.

That Budapest was destroyed by Russian tanks is tragic; but a greater tragedy had already occurred: the destruction of human decency."

The Escape, November of 1956

≈

It was time to act quickly, gather our family, and head for the West. We'd lost the revolution, and it would now mean jail for all of us, if not worse. Father announced that we needed to leave immediately. Little Nyuszi was already in Vienna, for Mother had sent a car for us girls as soon as the border opened. We had sent Nyuszi back alone, saying we could not yet leave. But now the Iron Curtain was closed, and we needed to rush through the cracks to get out.

Our little group of a dozen friends and neighbors headed for the border. We had a guide, who was a smuggler and knew the way. A young doctor and his wife had their infant child medicated so he would sleep through the trip. Edith and I helped carry the baby most of the way, and it was not easy walking. We walked, crawled, and dropped to the frozen ground any time we heard sounds or saw flares going up, lighting up the skies. It was slow going. Sometimes the flares created daylight in the night skies. We could only pray we would not be detected. It was the most terrifying experience of my life. My heart was beating furiously when we made it across the border, and it was a huge relief once we were safe on Austrian soil. Freedom—what joy! Some people kneeled down to kiss the ground.

We soon would see our beloved mother. Border guards were looking for refugees. They picked us up in our shattered state, and transported us to a school converted into a refugee camp, where we received hot tea, cookies, and warm blankets to rest on for the night. In the morning, we were escorted to the train station and sent to Vienna to reunite with Mother. It was so very exciting and almost dreamlike. Austria was a neutral country, and all signs of the war disappeared. Streets and stores were decorated for the holidays with so many lights we could not believe our eyes! The Austrians had great respect for the Hungarian freedom fighters, and helped anyone who needed it.

We finally arrived at Borseplatz 3, where both Mother and Aunt Mila lived after Mila's husband, Fano, had passed away. All of a sudden, our father had two wives: Mausi, the mother of his children, and Clara, the stepmother. He declared he loved them both equally. Within hours, a decision had to be made by the adults. The room was filled with family and friends, and the judge was Aunt Mila, who was the smallest but with the loudest voice. They were all sitting in enormous armchairs. Clara refused to step aside to enable the family to reunite. She was offered a very comfortable retirement, with housing and income for life. It would create an opportunity for Father to begin again with what he had left behind, factory and all. We girls were anxiously listening to the decision about our future, and Edith made her special plea to Clara, but there was no convincing her.

She would not let go of her man. Clara acted like the winning general of a battle. Shockingly, she announced to us all that she had been able to make contact with an uncle of Dad's who had emigrated to the USA in 1910. He was willing to sponsor our family in coming to Chicago, where he lived with his wife. Tragically, Clara had won. The whole idea was horrifying to us. We were ready to begin school in Vienna and resume life with our real parents. We would be a family again, never going far away from our beloved mother. But that was simply not to be.

Mother was never good at expressing her feelings; she was not much for kissing and hugging, but I always felt loved and cared for by her. She had such a joyful presence in spite of all her suffering. She later told me, "Just smile, and the world will smile with you!" It was a very simple philosophy, and one I continue to follow. She took us shopping for bras, which we had never had before. When she saw my broken front tooth, she immediately sent me to her dentist to get it fixed. I was so glad—I never wanted to smile because of that broken tooth. Now I could smile again!

After Edith heard the sad news, that Father was going to the USA with Clara and us three girls, she immediately decided to go back to Hungary. She refused to choose one parent over the other, and she also could not go off to the far away land knowing her dear boyfriend was just recovering from his bullet wounds from the revolution. She swore me to secrecy, for she had just enough time to be able to get across the border. After dark, I came home, but no Edith, which was rare. We always traveled the city together, had our meals in the many restaurants that offered us free food, but suddenly, I was alone.

It was very difficult for me that first night. I made excuses and went to bed, deciding that in the morning I would tell everyone that Edith had gone back home to Hungary. The family was stunned. But secretly, I had also decided to go back home myself, hopeful of bringing her back. I found a smuggler who was willing to take me. He went back and forth and made lots of money by bartering for people's jewelry in exchange for helping them escape.

We met at the train station after dark, and once the train stopped at the border, we started walking in the cold ice fields. He reminded me things were much more dangerous than in November when we had escaped. The Iron Curtain was now reinforced, and if caught, you would be shot. The worst part was when I needed to pee; I had to ask the smuggler to let me go behind a haystack and promise not to look. This was hard and mortifying, but necessary.

There was just a light layer of snow, and the wind blew in large swirls. It was freezing cold, but now I had warm coat, thanks to Mother, and warm gloves and a hat, even a wool scarf. I was ready to face the worst. We walked into the cold wind, then crawled and lay still, just like the first time. Flares lit up the skies, and we had to be very still when we heard dogs barking; the trip took a lot longer. We had taken a less traveled road, which he said was safer. Getting into the closed border was just as dangerous as getting out. Once we were near the first village, he arranged a horse-drawn wagon to take us to Mosonmagyarovar, where I was going, and there we parted.

Edith was relieved to see me but refused to return. She said I must now go back and take some students she was hiding in the house. They had been caught escaping and told that the next time they would be killed. I had to make sure they would make it! I felt like a hero rescuing these six students, who were older than my fourteen years. Edith also made me promise I would look after poor little Nyuszi, who needed my help, as she was going with Clara and Father.

The following night, the seven of us started out on our long cold journey; I was now the leader, showing the way, knowing when to lie still and when to slip into ditches to wait until everything was quiet and dark. The trip took a long time, for I wanted to be very sure we got out—I had a mission. After hours of slow creeping on all fours, occasionally running, then back to creeping, we made it across the border. For me, it was the third time. Once we were at a safe distance from "no-man's-land," we were so delighted that we let out a big shout to relieve all the tension. We even made plans to go to Australia together, far away from here!

However, my plans changed dramatically. As soon as we were spotted by the Austrian border guards we were taken to a place for hot drinks and cookies. They called Mother and told her I was safe, and proceeded to drive me all the way to the city and Mother's house in the middle of the night.

The next day Father and Clara were ready to go to the US Embassy to apply for immigration visas for the four of us. I took Nyuszi out of school. We all had our pictures taken and were sent to a local camp where other families were already awaiting their departure for the new land, the new life far away. I looked upon all this as a big adventure.

My dreams were finally realized. After all, we would be in the USA—where people drive big cars and have machines to do all the work—and that's the place I wanted to go! The camp was nice, and we made friends, played cards, and rode around on trains and streetcars. Everything was available to us for free, even food and drinks in designated restaurants. After several days in a camp just outside of the city, we were transferred to a different location, much further away. We said our goodbyes to Mother and Aunt Mila, and were on our way.

News spread quickly through the camp. President Eisenhower had announced that all Hungarian families would be in the USA by Christmas. We were excited! It was mid-December, and in the town we were in, the shops were brimming with presents. There were enough lights to light up the whole world. On every street, music was playing, even outdoors. Could it get any better? Imagine coming from a Hungarian town where most street lights had burned out long ago, and no one had bothered to replace them. It was a town where streets were dark, and shops turned out their lights at closing to save power and hide how poor they were. In Austria, however, during this holiday season, shops were showing an infinite variety of goods. Shining packages decorated every corner of every window, tempting the most discriminating buyer to stop and have a look inside. At this happy time, our names were finally posted on the bulletin board, which meant saying goodbye to many new friends, and packing our meager belongings for this long trip. I could hardly contain my excitement!

Our turn came on December 22, 1956, when we were driven by bus to the military plane with the American flag and "USA" painted on it; we all wanted our picture taken by this sign. It was a four-engine transport plane, and in it, we began our journey to the "land of opportunity," which offered freedom and a new life.

Arriving in the USA

〜

It was a scary flight. Cabins in military planes are not fully pressurized. Clara was unable to breath, so they gave her an oxygen mask, which she needed the whole flight. As we traveled through dark skies late into the night, the pilot announced there was a blizzard on the whole east coast, from Maine to New York. We would have to stop to refuel and wait out the storm in Greenland. We were tired and sleepy, but there was hot coffee, tea, and cookies in the waiting room, so we settled down with the other stranded passengers. Someone recognized Louis Armstrong, who was on a different flight, also waiting out the big storm. He had his trumpet with him, and when he found out we were Hungarian refugees, he decided to serenade us, playing his trumpet, singing, and even taking requests. That woke us up, and we had an impromptu party. We were all singing Christmas songs and learning new English words to old favorites, and it made the wait pleasant. When we were finally able to return to the plane and continue our journey, we were reenergized! What a wonderful way to spend an otherwise dull stopover. The rest of the flight was uneventful. We arrived at the New Jersey military airport where buses were lined up to take us to Camp Kilmer for further initiation and medical exams.

If the lights of Vienna had astonished us, the miracle we saw in the short drive from the airport to the camp was amazing. It was as if a magician had gotten loose and created this dazzling display. Everywhere you looked, there were lights of many colors, and all the homes were decorated, even the roofs. It looked like a winter wonderland in the heavy snow! It was Christmas Eve, and we had our best ever present: we were in the safest country, the "land of opportunity," the land of freedom and peace. What a great way to celebrate our first Christmas in our new country. I was so grateful that my dreams were beginning to become reality.

We settled into life at camp. It was filled with bunk beds and strange food and many people everywhere, but it was a temporary situation. We had English classes daily, of which I took advantage. During the two months we spent at camp, we learned to fill-up on foods familiar to us, mostly rolls and butter and eggs. The bread we found inedible, for it looked like white cotton and tasted the same! Peanut butter was unknown to us, and so were many of the food combinations. Because of Clara's asthma, we were detained for a longer period than most. Officials wanted to be sure she was not bringing any strange disease into the country.

Nyuszi and I had learned how to use an electric iron instead of a coal heated one. We learned how to press men's shirts as well as our blouses. The few things we had now looked clean and pressed.

I met a young man who took my fancy. He was an Elvis Presley look-alike—tall, dark, and handsome—from Budapest. When he found out about the resemblance, he even learned to play the guitar. I was very much in love. We watched movies at night in the movie theater at camp and held hands, even kissed. He was shipped out quickly to a good university, and I missed him, but we kept in touch by mail for a while. His name was Jesse. I had left Europe as a girl and arrived in the USA as a woman.

In spite of the failed attempt to free the country from the oppressing Russian invaders, over a hundred thousand of us had left Hungary and the communist rule to find freedom. There were volunteers from the community who took us into New York. This was an unforgettable event, the most remarkable part being the many lights and people. I loved the beautiful store windows, and was amazed by a trip to the automat, where we were allowed to try something from the machine. People came and went at the camp. We became friends with a family from our hometown who were also going to Chicago, which meant we could remain in touch after the camp.

Finally the day came when we were able to leave. Father contacted Uncle Steve, whom we had never met, and told him when our train would arrive at Chicago Union Station. After an amazing train ride, we arrived midafternoon, and Uncle Steve and his wife came to pick us up in their little Nash Rambler, which was pink and gray. There were four of us and two of them, and his car was made for only four people; somehow we squeezed in. We were amazed by the tall buildings we passed in downtown Chicago. Uncle Steve drove us to their home, which was our new temporary headquarters. From the station to their house in Humboldt Park, we got to see a lot of the city and the skyline, and even caught a small glimpse of the lake. I loved it all, and could not get enough of my new city.

Even though we were related, Uncle Steve and his wife, Aunt Paula, were total strangers to us, people who had a very different lifestyle. They'd never had children, and lived modestly in a simple frame home with a lovely garden. They had left their home as teenagers, met at Ellis Island, and married—he from Hungary, she from Germany. They had settled down, and he'd worked as a carpenter's apprentice, later moving up to be the master, never really moving around much. They were just waiting for retirement, when they would move to Florida. We had very little in common, but I learned a lot fast just walking around the neighborhood and going in to stores. Every day was a learning experience: taking the streetcar, roaming the streets, learning about American money and its value. We soon met other Hungarians through the local church. We enjoyed these new friends and began attending events with them, mostly Hungarian programs and dances. Before long, we met another family from our hometown who had lived in Chicago for many years. They helped us find our first apartment, and helped Nyuszi and I get enrolled in schools. They even assisted in finding jobs for Father and Clara.

Our first apartment was very nice. It was two bedrooms, and we furnished it from a Hungarian-owned furniture store on credit. We lived with that same furniture for all of Dad's and Clara's lives.

Having been raised by nuns, a very conservative governess, and Mother, I knew how important it was to be a virgin at the time you married. There was no question about this. No self-respecting girl would risk messing it up. Still, I had no clue as to what they did, for I was so naive. No one had ever educated me about sex, men, or even menstruation. I only knew kissing was OK and was as far as one could allow a boy to go. They mostly kissed just my hand, but in a very special case, the lips were OK. Maybe that was not all bad: I experienced romance on my own and learned the way of the world very slowly and carefully.

Mostly girls in the new world knew so much more about sex and being around boys. I had little experience, having gone to all-girls schools where I had little contact with the opposite sex. My only exposure was dance school, where we had to interact with boys. Boys at thirteen and fourteen are just kids, and we girls were looking at the more mature young men we liked but with whom we had little contact. It was in Chicago where I first had a chance to really dance with men. Suddenly, I had many chances to interact and play: going to the beach with a large group, playing soccer or beach volleyball, bicycling, and playing tennis. I even had my first unescorted trip to Washington, DC with two college students and my much older friend, Mary. It was a weekend trip, but it meant so much to be away from parents on a road trip to the capital.

We girls and the boys had separate rooms; we all enjoyed many new experiences including going to museums, where we learned firsthand about the young history of this great country.

Mary, my new friend, was the one who introduced me to two young Hungarians who were arriving from Detroit to attend Roosevelt University. She helped them find housing, and she was hoping to get the attention of the man I ended up marrying. Once she realized he was only interested in me, she stopped calling me, and we grew apart, no longer friends. In retrospect, she might have been a better partner for him and his many problems; but I was only eighteen, and have my two wonderful children from our union, for whom I am grateful.

I went to meet the director of Lakeview High School; the physical education teacher was also present because he happened to be of Hungarian decent. They advised me to start in the first grade and go through all eight grades to get the very basics of the language, reminding me how difficult English was for someone of my background. I followed through with this suggestion, although I was hugely humiliated by sitting in a tiny desk with six-year-olds, moving up weekly to a higher level. It was terrible being made fun of, and I felt like a total failure. I was very good at gym and physical activities, but our physical education classes consisted of stupid baseball, which made no sense to me, and I never wanted to learn it in the first place. I was a good gymnast, but they did not do any gymnastics in gym classes.

Finally, I finished with the eight grades and was able to start high school. It was spring, and everyone was already paired up and cliques existed. There was no room for a foreign newcomer who they referred to as a "DP" (displaced person). I felt alone, and began to think, was it my appearance? I had always thought I was attractive to look at from the way guys looked at me and the whistles I had received on the beach. But now I questioned everything. I had little free time since I was enrolled in an English-for-foreign-students class, held a job delivering groceries from the greengrocer nearby, and was struggling to keep up with the high school homework, which only seemed difficult because of the language barrier.

Then summer arrived, and I now had many friends. We could walk to the beach or take a streetcar if we were lazy, and play on the waterfront with our friends. Some of them even had cars, and we could go on outings to explore far away beaches, get to know the surrounding areas, and even go dancing in the evenings. I was able to work longer hours, but the money I made went to the common household. Clara handled all the finances, so we had to ask her for money for the bus, or cigarettes, or coke, and I never had much.

When my first year of high school ended, I found out I could work full-time by going to school two full days a week. Then I would go to school "after work" on the other three days. This allowed me to get a job with Bankers Life Insurance. They let me take two days off for school and continue the night schooling. I was gone all the time, barely spending any time at home, which was good for me but hard for poor Nyuszi. She was enrolled in the nearest Catholic school and would go on to Catholic high school. She made many friends, and learned English fast and even learned the lyrics to all the popular songs. The first day she went to school and was asked her name, she proudly announced, "Piroska Ludmilla," and received a big laugh. She then said the only English name that she remembered, "Betty," and from that day on she was called Betty.

Before long, it was our second Christmas in our new country. There was a frenzy of decorating and shopping, and everyone was busy writing cards and having open houses. I had trouble relating to all this commerce attached to Christmas, my favorite holiday.

But let me digress. Christmas was always the most special holiday for me because it coincided with my name day on December 24th, a day we celebrated even more than birthdays in Hungary. We observed Christmas with ancient ceremonies, some dating back to pre-Christian times. These were so ingrained in our lives that we continued on, even during communism, in spite of the rules forbidding them. They were celebrated like country fairs in the USA. There was music, dancing, rides, and very special foods connected to each holiday. Saint Steven, the first king of Hungary, who settled the nomad Huns in the central European valleys and brought Christianity to the country, had a very elaborate name-day celebration. It fell at the end of August, the time of harvest.

The harvest celebration came from pagan times, though with some Christian symbols, and there was always plenty of food and drink. There usually was a roasted pig on the pit and many tasty baked goods. There were fires burning and young people dancing around them while music was played by gypsies in their colorful attire.

The gypsies still lived like nomads, roaming the countryside, never settling in one place for long. They were still hunter/gatherers (which in most case meant gathering other people's property and living off the work of others who planted and worked the land). Their kids did not attend school. And gypsies were feared by hardworking farmers because they stole their livestock and had no respect for personal property. They were also fearless fighters on fast horses who could rarely be brought to justice.

During communism, holidays became the worker's celebrations. On May 1st, we celebrated the party's win over the previous government, whose representatives had been executed or imprisoned for life. It was a big day to showcase Russia's military might, with marching soldiers in fancy uniforms and lumbering tanks with big numbers and guns. All school-aged children were required to march in their little "uttoro" uniforms, which meant "paving the way." We had to march with our red kerchiefs tied around our necks, sometimes freezing in the cold early spring breezes. We had to stand through the long-winded speakers who spent hours praising each other, Stalin, and Lenin. In turn, we had to sing the communist songs praising them as our saviors. Once the much-hated ceremony ended, we hurried to the park where there would be plenty of good food, rides, music, and dancing.

This celebration had been quite different before the communist era. Young men erected maypoles in front of their intended's houses and decorated them with colorful ribbons. When the young lady awoke in the morning and found a maypole in front of her window, it meant there was going to be a wedding in the near future. (Of course, if there were several young ladies in the family, it could get confusing when there was only one pole.) The maypole ceremony dates back to long ago, when the pole was often used to start a family home.

Another ancient holiday was October 31st, "All Souls Day," celebrated all over the world. Almost every culture has a version of this holiday. We carried lanterns and candles or luminaries to the cemetery, where they were lit on every grave; people greeted each other and celebrated their ancestors and prayed for their souls to go to the next existence safely. This also involved fasting, cleansing, and purification, very much like Yum Kippur in the Jewish religion.

A Pilgrimage

〜

One of my memories from an All Saints Day pilgrimage is so vivid it seems like yesterday. We awoke long before sunrise and had a little satchel ready with a sandwich and some apples. We began our pilgrimage to the celebrated saint's birthplace, a town where the remains were kept in a crypt at the church. We walked for hours, stopping at a stream for water or a bathroom break or sometimes just to rest and have a bite of our goodies. After hours of walking, usually barefoot, our feet were aching. We joined the other folks coming from many different parts, some walking for days. We formed a large group, all gathering for the same purpose. Some of the older, sicker folks were crawling on their hands and knees, covered in dust. They believed that if they made it to the end and gave their tired, worn bodies as an offering to this saint, they would regain their health and wellbeing. They believed that just by making the pilgrimage their wishes would be granted.

The crowd arrived in the little village and found it prepared for this event. Vendors lined the streets with their offerings. There were rosaries, amulets, and flowers to take to the church. There were sellers of gingerbread, cotton candy, roast pork, and fried bread. I loved the excitement of the trip, watching the sunrise bring light to the day, warming the air and drying the dew as it slowly evaporated. As we grew ever closer, we started removing our sweaters and walked a little faster in anticipation of the scene awaiting us. Priests appeared out of nowhere carrying a large cross, and the prayers began with hundreds of voices saying Hail Marys. Some hymns were sung, more prayers were said; it was hypnotic. You could not help feeling elated and carried away when you saw the strong faith exhibited by this large mass of humanity. Once we reached our destination, which was the tiny church in the middle of the town square, we squeezed in as tightly as possible and made our way to the gold-encrusted coffin of the saint. Each person had a chance to kiss the coffin and to say a prayer or make a wish before moving on. The strong smell of burning candles and incense mingled and stayed with me long after I left. The intensity of feelings surrounded me with awe.

Sometimes there were rides, jugglers, gypsy musicians, and even a music box with a live monkey, which was trained to pick pockets. You had to guard what you did not want to lose. The monkey was clever—dancing and even lifting his small hat off to the ladies—and he was dressed like a sailor. The music box was operated by his owner who would sing raucous sailor songs to keep the audience's attention. We would drop some coins into the hat on the ground and laugh as we watched. Once we had seen it all, said our prayers, made our wishes, and collected some souvenirs, it was time to go home.

These events were woven into country life, and you had to make your pilgrimages on foot, not on bicycles or horseback or any other mode of transport. This may have been good for our health. Once home, tired and dusty, we were ready for a bath and long slumber. As a child, I remember counting the days until these holidays arrived; to begin, once again, the journey to a new destination.

Christmases Passed

≈

Christmas remained my all-time favorite holiday. One of the best I remember was very early in my life, when we were still a loving family with Mother, Father, Louise, and our grandparents in our beautiful home. Edith and I were kept entertained by our governess while preparations were being made in the salon, anxiously waiting for the little bell to ring that indicated Christmas had arrived.

It was magical! The double doors would fly open to reveal the most beautiful floor-to-ceiling tree—all decorated and shining with dozens of lighted candles on its branches—and presents under the tree. It was the magic of the moment: the smell of pine mingled with burning candles, the tinkle of bells. It was as if the angels had disappeared leaving only their shining light, and all of us were basking in the glow.

Christmas was not about the presents. Instead it was about the feeling of love and security I felt toward all the people I cared about, our loving family, together with happy smiling faces. My heart would overflow with joy!

There were some other wonderful holidays, but none stand out like the Christmas when I was only three years old. All other Christmases pale in comparison. I never had that beautiful, warm feeling again until I had my own children; then we created that warm family feeling with just the few of us together, still trying to preserve the essence of the holiday.

Emery Homor, My First Husband

~

I met Emery through my friend, Mary Kortvelyesi, in the fall of 1958. He and his friend, Nandi (Ferdinand), were both sickly, skinny, and pale. They were undernourished and had poor teeth, but were strikingly smart, well-read, and ready to start back to university after a long hiatus. They often came over for a good home-cooked meal, and sometimes asked me out to the beach or a movie. I was always obliged to take little Betty with me.

How my little sister became Betty is another story. The first day she went to school and was asked her name, she loudly announced, "Piroska," and there was laughter in the room. The teacher could not repeat it, so she asked her what she wanted to be called, and the only name that came to her was Betty. From that day on, it was her American name.

The four of us spent time together, just casually as friends. Emery told me the story of his life: How as a third-year law student in the prestigious Pazmany Peter Law School in Budapest, he was arrested by the AVO. He was falsely charged and tortured, unable to give up information he did not even have. They totally broke his spirit and stole all his dignity. The prisoners were treated so inhumanly that many died. They had spent their days and nights in dingy cells, jammed together with ten to fifteen men. They slept on a concrete floor, and their only facility was a bucket for elimination. The food they were given was a warm liquid with some pieces of potato skins floating in it and sometimes pieces of lard, which was treasured. Many of them died of various diseases, malnutrition, scurvy, or other problems; sometimes the scars from beatings and tortures became infected and were not treated.

Emery's skin suffered, and he looked emaciated. After a mock trial he was thrown into a solitary cell. The only fortunate part in this situation was that he could read all he wanted, and he read as much as the daylight allowed. In the five years he spent in solitary, he had been given all the classics, which were a great source of knowledge from literary greats. He became well-read.

The prisoners devised a code by which they communicated with each other at night, a type of Morse code done by knocking. Emery knew when someone was carried out dead or beaten unconscious or taken to the prison hospital, but that was all he knew of the world for those five years.

Then, suddenly, in 1956, the prison doors flew open, freeing all inmates. He had a quick reunion with his family and announced that he was immediately escaping to the West with many of his friends. It was a difficult parting with his aging parents, sister, and brother, but he knew there was no choice. He, his friend, and some other former prisoners headed for the border as a group. Among them were doctors, lawyers, engineers, students, and other educated people, as well as those who had formerly managed the affairs of the country and survived. It was a huge loss to Hungary. Over one hundred thousand citizens departed, mostly from the former middle class.

Once Emery arrived in the USA, the land of opportunity, the two friends decided they had had enough schooling. They were offered scholarships to the best universities, which they foolishly declined. They wanted to make their fortunes fast after losing all those productive years in prison. Finally, they were sent to Detroit to work. After a year spent washing walls at the Henry Ford Hospital, earning minimal wages and eating dog food to save on groceries, they were ready to resume their studies if any scholarships were left. They were lucky to get into Roosevelt University in Chicago. This is how we met.

Emery and Nandi moved into our neighborhood. They took public transportation to school, and both of them worked at the school library. They lived on canned dog food, which they found very nourishing, tasty, and cheap. We had them over for family meals often, which they devoured greedily no matter what it was.

In nice weather, we played soccer, tennis, and swam off the rocks in Lake Michigan. We also went to the movies and studied. We lived just a block from the lake and park, which provided us with recreation and a safe place right in the Belmont Harbor area.

One night, we were out drinking and dancing and stayed out too late. When Emery took me home, it was after midnight, and I was locked out. I knocked and knocked on the apartment door. When Father finally came to the door, he said I had not come home on time, so he could not let me in. Emery then started to negotiate with Father. Suddenly, Emery announced that he had asked for my hand in marriage, and that was what we had been celebrating.

That was not the case, but Father liked the idea, so he opened the door and gave us each a big hug of approval. I was engaged without having a say about it! I was going to confess in the morning and tell Father it was just an excuse Emery had made up, but then I decided it might be an easy way out of my prison, so I went along with the plan. We had an engagement party with some friends, and then set a date for our wedding—over Thanksgiving weekend in the fall of 1959, only months after we had met.

I was eighteen and about to marry a man of thirty-three. We were both still in school and struggling financially. After completing my high school degree, I enrolled in the school of the Art Institute of Chicago, an amazing school in the bowels of the museum, which seemed like a subbasement, but we had great teachers. I loved being a student there and adored studying art.

Life was tough; I did not know how to cook, only how to boil an egg or a hot dog. Dog food was out of the question for me, so I lived on cigarettes and coke. We both smoked heavily in those dark days—it was so glamorous. Still, I knew I had made a mistake as soon as I walked down the aisle. The weather was dreadful, pouring rain, and I wore a white brocade dress with a small crown of flowers and a veil.

I did not feel special or loved, only frightened of what was to come. Poor little sister, Betty, envied me, for she wanted out of the prison as well. It was a very small wedding: Betty, Clara, and Father. The only guest other than Nandi, the best man, was Tommy, a relative on Clara's side. It was held in Winfield, Illinois, where the resident priest was Hungarian and could communicate well with us.

Back at the house, we had a glass of champagne and cake, and some friends came over to congratulate us. The only wedding gift we received was a set of crystal ashtrays, which we put to good use right away.

Housing was decided the following way: I was to move in with Emery, my husband, while his roommate and friend, Nandi, would rent my room at my parent's house. It was a simple arrangement, but not very wise; Betty was only fourteen, a lovely teenager, while Nandi was a man of thirty-three.

I wanted Betty to go back to Vienna and live with Mother, to get away from this potentially dangerous situation.

Letter to Mother

~

Dearest Mother,

You will be hearing from Clara and Dad. Do not respond until you hear the truth from me; it will not come from them. Now that I am married, I see things a little differently, especially your situation in our family.

I love you and miss you very much and look forward to the times we can reunite and get to know each other as adults and friends.

When we got Father to leave home and cross into Austria, we envisioned our family reuniting, and the five of us starting our life together, finally, after all those years of separation. It must have been terribly difficult for you to know how close your little girls were geographically, and yet we could not make contact for so many years.

When we arrived in your home with Clara in tow, we had nothing but the necessities provided by the Red Cross. Our dreams and hopes were so palpable. I know Dad's choice was not based on his feelings for Clara, nor his lack of love for you. His final decision was purely based on his righteousness, for he was not able to leave this very sickly woman alone after she had spent the most horrific years with him, the years when everything had been taken from us. He never even knew that Clara had not lifted a finger after we had become destitute. She simply lay down, sick, telling us girls that from now on we were going to do all the work, which had been done by the help before. Her mother, who was both epileptic and old, was running the household along with our help. Money was scarce, sometimes nonexistent, and we had to use our wits to provide. Although she was only nine, Edith was very clever. She leased land, which the two of us worked, sometimes with Father pitching in. We grew corn and sugar beets for sale, which provided some income. To feed the wood-burning stoves, we collected wood in the forest and carried it home on the only remaining bicycle we had between four of us.

Clara began selling our belongings behind Father's back and then accused us of stealing them. Father was so gullible that he not only believed her, but we were also sometimes beaten half to death for it. We suffered for many things of her doing. Edith and I got such beatings that we could not sit for days. One by one, his handmade shoes were sold, as well as his custom shirts, silk robes, and other clothes, for Clara needed money to buy the wine that she loved and was addicted to. Her doctor was very close to her, providing the many medications to which she was also addicted. He often came to the house and spent hours discussing books with her, exchanging reading material, and arguing about the political situation.

It may sound silly, but now that I am married, I miss you even more than ever. I would like to lay my head on your shoulder, have your loving arms enfold me, and to hear you say, "It will be OK, don't cry," like you did when I was a little girl. I still have such vivid memories of the happy days, when we were a family, before the war, before Betty, before the end. You probably realized that Edith was the victim of Father's poor decision. Out of her love for you, she could not take sides, leave you behind, and come with us to the USA. She also knew that she could not stay with you and hurt him. She felt that going back home was her only choice.

Life was rather difficult for me as well. After two and a half months at Camp Kilmer in New Jersey, we finally left for Chicago to meet

Uncle Steve and Aunt Paula. They lived a very primitive lifestyle, as he had left home at seventeen and made his way on freighter to the USA. He met his German wife, who was sixteen, at Ellis Island. They married, and eked out a living without education. He had learned the carpentry trade and worked in a small shop most of his life, saving every penny for retirement, which sadly they never got to enjoy. The two of them pinched pennies, never had children, and did not trust banks; so when the four of us arrived and moved into their very neat, small house, it was like living in Lilliput Land. They were both short, and everything in the house was minute; our very presence filled the space! They drove a very small, pink Nash Rambler, a tiny little car, and Aunt Paula never learned to drive.

The two of us girls started school immediately, and I managed to get a job in a greengrocers about a mile away from the house, which allowed me to be out of the way most of the time. Father and Clara were not able to get jobs right away due to the language problem, but with the help of the church and the Hungarian community, we got an apartment and furnished it on credit from the local dealer. At last, we were able to move into our own apartment on the north side of Chicago.

Money was needed, so I worked long hours and weekends, got a better paying job at Bankers Life Insurance Company, and continued taking English classes in the evenings. Television and newspapers were excellent learning tools, but I had little time to utilize them. I was still going to high school for a degree. It was very busy, and I had no time for fun, like other teenagers.

It was not long after we moved into our lovely apartment on Pinegrove and Addison, just a block from the lake, the park, and the harbor, that I met my future husband. He proposed under duress, and I never even had a chance to refuse. Father and Clara were delighted to have me off their hands. Our wedding was a sad event, in pouring rain, and my white brocade dress (ready-made off the rack at Goldblatt's) was soaking wet when I walked down the aisle. We only had the two witnesses at the wedding.

As soon as I moved out of my parents, my room was rented to Emery's roommate, Nandi, who was also thirty-three; Betty was only fourteen, a ravishing teenager. She was totally serving Father and Clara—cooking, shopping, and cleaning for them—since they now had employment and she was just going to school. Her life was not easy, and suddenly she was getting all this love and attention from a much older man, which was flattering. Before long, he seduced her. Emery and I were not even allowed to contact them because Emery had had a big fight with Clara and Dad about the lack of supervision. He was told to leave and not return. I am so concerned for Betty; she is again the victim of her circumstances. She is a very beautiful young girl who has a very bleak future with a much older husband with whom she has nothing in common. Even I suffered from the huge age gap in my marriage, but just imagine how it will effect this very young, naive girl who should be playing with dolls still, not having an affair with a much older, strange man. Mommy, please help! If she can come and stay with you, this could go away, and she might have a chance for a happier life! I love you very much, and look forward to our future.

Your daughter,
Eva

Regrettably, in spite of my efforts, there was little Mother could do to change the events.

Betty and Nandi Get Married
(She Sixteen, He Thirty-Five)

~

As it turned out, they waited until Betty turned sixteen and could legally marry in Illinois. Soon after, Nandi was transferred to Pittsburgh, the corporate headquarters, where he became the comptroller at H.J. Heinz Company, a position he held to the end of his life.

She was an unhappy bride, very young, naive, and beautiful. He was a man of the world, for he had been the privileged child of an aristocratic family. He had worked for the CIA, was arrested, and spent several years behind bars as a political prisoner before being freed by the 1956 uprising and revolution. He was good at his job but had no idea how to be a husband; it was a difficult marriage.

Our life was full. Emery was in school, working and studying. I soon realized we could not make ends meet on the meager part-time incomes we earned, so I quit school in order to work full-time and bring home a decent salary on which we could survive. I got a secretarial job at Material Service, a Division of General Dynamics, in the coal department. I was one of two women in a sea of men.

We had our own building on West Washington Street in downtown Chicago. It was a direct commute: I walked a few blocks to the elevated, and it ended in the subway, from which it was only a few-blocks walk to the office. I enjoyed all the attention I received from the men. They had me repeat words I mispronounced, and were always asking me for things with names I had trouble saying. It was a good experience. My immediate boss was Byron Weil, whose executive father was still on the payroll and made the trip to work every morning in a limousine for lack of anything else to do.

Byron and his dad sent me out to get special meals, and I sometimes had to go a long way to get what they desired. I learned to type on my own—not very fast, but enough—and I developed good people skills. However, I had to take a lot of ribbing from the men in the workplace, who were constantly making fun of my accent.

I got pregnant very shortly after I quit school. Emery called my ob-gyn and told him we couldn't have a child now, so we needed an abortion. I was in hospital just overnight with a "miscarriage." I could never forgive Emery! I so wanted a child, and he just was not ready to deal with family. As it turned out, I made him promise that I could keep the next pregnancy, but it had to be on his timing. I was on the pill, which in those days was extremely strong.

Finally, he finished law school at Loyola, while I was working two part-time jobs on top of my full-time one. My days were filled. From the office, I would rush over to any one of the hotels where I was either a "hat-and-coat-check girl" in cool weather, or a receptionist/greeter in warmer months. They notified me where to show up for work. I went between the Ambassador hotels, the Bismarck Hotel, the Palmer House, and wherever else they had private parties. I was asked to work the night shift, and lived on cigarettes, Coca Cola, and an occasional sandwich if money allowed. The highlight of this very low-wage job was meeting some famous entertainers, like Liz Taylor at the Ambassador East when she was married to Eddy Fisher, and George Gobel at the Palmer House Empire Room. I enjoyed seeing some entertaining shows.

I saved every penny I could for the baby I so wanted. And finally, after Emery passed the Illinois bar, I was allowed to get pregnant. It happened very soon, and before long I was showing a little bump of a belly. I worked through the eight months of pregnancy and was given a delightful going-away party at Trader Vic's in the Palmer House. I had a very large rum punch and felt the effect all the way home! Now I was a lady of leisure, getting ready for my first baby and preparing for motherhood.

Charmaine Is Born, 1963

≈

With my little savings, I was able to get a few necessities. We made the move to a nice family-friendly neighborhood in the Rogers Park area, just north of Touhy and east of Western avenues, near a lovely park—with a petting zoo—called Indian Boundary. It had a nice playground, and I knew I was going to spend a lot of time there. My baby girl, Charmaine, was helped into the world by Dr. Glenner. He wanted to go on vacation and said he would induce me if she was not out by the tenth of April, so my little baby girl arrived as planned by the doc. We name her Charmaine. I was delighted and so was her father. We were both beside ourselves! I immediately announced that I was going to nurse her, but in those days it was discouraged rather than supported. The moment my milk came in, I was waiting for the nurse to bring my little baby, but it did not happen; so I walked down to the nursery and found they were bottle feeding all the newborn infants. I immediately created a scene, shouting that I wanted to feed my baby. I had Emery take me home after two nights (a week was the norm in those days). I wanted out because it was such a struggle to connect with my baby at each feeding before they stuck a bottle into her mouth. She was a lovely baby who slept a lot, which allowed me to do a lot of work around the house. Sometimes I would spend time just staring at this beautiful new life—the miracle of it all!

Even though the laundry room was three floors down, in the basement, I trudged there to wash the diapers as well as all the other laundry. There were little hand-knit and crocheted clothes I had made for her, as well as the bedding and our own clothes.

I carried Charmaine in one arm while lugging all the laundry and detergent up and down many times a day.

Of course we only had one car, which Emery used to commute to work. If I had an appointment and had to have the car, I had to get up extra early, dress the baby, and drive my husband to work. Then I also had to pick him up after work. It was hard, but it brought me so much joy to have a real-live doll to dress and feed and take care of. I loved every minute of it! Being a mother was the biggest joy I ever experienced in life. As soon as Betty saw Charmaine, she declared, "She is sweet as a cookie," and the nickname stuck—my little Cookie!

Life was a joy, and I did not mind the work or the fact I was so isolated and had no one to turn to for advice. Before long, I began to make friends in the park. We all had the same issues, and so I organized a weekly playgroup in each other's homes and a babysitting exchange, which was very successful from the start. We all needed time away from baby, and we could exchange information and get advice on raising children, other than from Dr. Spock. (I read all I could of his books and found them very helpful.)

Before long, Emery had planned a family vacation to the mountains he had missed so much. He made all the plans: we were to ride the train from Chicago to Denver in the dome car, and stay at the Stanley Hotel at Estes Park, Colorado. I was excited! I planned all I was going to need for the trip, started packing, and off we went by train on our first family vacation. The hotel was wonderful, the food very nice, and we did a lot of hiking in the mountains, even climbing Pike's Peak. However, I was feeling sick the whole time, nauseated. They fed me dark chocolate for altitude sickness, but it turned out to be morning sickness, for I was expecting again. I believe Rod was conceived in the mountains of Colorado. He started growing and kicking after we returned back home. This was a much more active pregnancy, and Rod proved to be a much larger baby at birth. Also, he had a much bigger appetite right from the start!

I was so happy to have the perfect family—a boy and a girl. We had to move to a bigger apartment to accommodate both the crib and a bed for little Cookie. I found the perfect apartment, not far, on the ground floor this time, where the laundry was again in the basement but not several floors away. I delighted walking my two lovely babies in the stroller to the park, or to visit my newly acquired friends. In the first apartment, we met the Crowleys, who became good friends of the family. In our second apartment, we became friends with the Seitz family; Roger was an architect and Jan was his wife, and we soon became good friends. They also had two children: Steven, the eldest, and Rodi, the younger girl. We kept up our friendship after they moved to a lovely home in Evanston, and they often invited us over on playdates.

At this point, my brother-in-law, Nandi, found out he had been transferred to Pittsburgh, the national headquarters for H.J. Heinz Company where he was a controller. He packed and was ready to go. Poor Betty could not even imagine life alone in a strange city without any family or friends. She made the move with him, and when I went to visit them with my two little ones, I found she had her son Michael but no friends or anyone to turn to for advice or help.

She then returned to Chicago while he remained in Pittsburgh, and they never divorced. However, her struggles now began in earnest.

Being a single mom with no education and raising her son Michael had not been easy for Betty. The only joy she looked forward to came every winter during tax season, when Emery, who worked for a CPA firm, was overwhelmed with work. Betty and I would pack up the kids and drive down to Florida for a winter break—sunshine and ocean. Our Florida trips were also a good break for my children and me. We escaped from the cold winter weather, and had fresh fruit off the trees. We lived frugally in motels as we traveled, for the children were young and had not yet started school.

I was anxious to start working again; money was in short supply, and most kids were in preschool anyway. After checking around, I found a wonderful French school that started at preschool and went up to eighth grade. It was a nearby location and not terribly expensive, and I enrolled both Cookie and Rod. My hope was that they would learn French early in life and this would make them more interesting people. They liked the school, and I liked the teachers, so it was a win-win! I also landed a job close by, so while they were in school, I could earn. Emery, on the other hand, did not like the high price of the school for two, and he decided we needed to buy a home instead. So the search began: Evanston, Wilmette, and on up the North Shore until we found a lovely home we could afford in Lake Bluff, the furthest north suburb.

Our First Home

≈

Moving to our first home was an adventure! To finally have a garden with trees, to be able to grow vegetables and herbs, to play in the grass barefoot—it was all a dream come true for me. We met our friendly neighbors, who came bearing gifts to welcome us. The children quickly found playmates of their own. The house was only a short walk from our beloved Lake Michigan's beach, where we spent every warm, sunny day from morning till night. School was also a short walk for the kids. They liked making new friends and playing in the park, and soon I started both of them skating. This was my favorite sport, but I never really had a chance to learn and develop my skills, so I started my children young.

Cookie enjoyed it and learned quickly. The first time Rod stepped on the ice, he just ran across, amazing me. He was a natural at any sport he tried, and skating was just one of them.

While the children were in school, I started teaching yoga, since all my neighbors were amazed that I was so good at doing it, and they wanted to learn. Soon my neighbor Mary Clark found a suitable hall where I could teach and even earn some money.

The first time Rod played tennis with his father, he won. Emery never wanted to play with him again. Emery was never athletic and was somewhat jealous of his son being so good at every sport he played.

When Rod was asked to join the local hockey team, it meant lots of practice was necessary. Cookie took up figure skating on my encouragement, and enjoyed the pretty little costumes as well as the ballet classes that were required for skating. She was living out my early dreams! It became my full-time job just taking them to their after-school practices, especially since hockey required one parent being present at all times because of the chance of injuries. Emery was seldom available, for he was a workaholic, leaving early, and coming home late. He only took weekends off to work in the yard, and sometimes spent time with the kids, but not often.

We got permission to skate early in the morning at the Lake Forest College's rink. This meant that I drove them to the rink before school, and they ate breakfast in the car. Then they skated for an hour before I drove them on to school. After school, they could walk over to the Bath and Tennis Club in town to get in even more skating practice. It was a demanding sport, not just for the kids but for the parents as well. However, when Cookie reached high school age, she decided skating was too demanding for a normal life and gave it up. Rod wanted to continue hockey, but at this point I was getting ready to divorce Emery.

The Divorce

≈

I finally got up the courage to tell Emery it was over. We had been married eight years when I first told him I wanted a divorce. He threatened to take the kids from me, and because he was an attorney, I believed he could. Only years later did I realize it was just big talk—he could not. Divorce was tough for all of us, and the hardest part was most of our friends sided with him; I was no longer included in invitations, but he was. He became desirable, where I became a threat to many women. We did start a trend, however; after our splitting as a couple, several of our friends also did.

We decided to sell the big house (by now we lived in a large bi-level home in Lake Bluff), and I found a small ranch on the main street in town with a beautiful garden at a good price. Emery was entitled to half the assets of the house, which allowed him to get what he needed. I knew I had to work, and was offered a job by a friend who was the owner of Peterson Interiors. I started to work while running a household with two teenagers, a dog named Ginger, and a cat who ran away. It became apparent that I needed to go back to school, so I enrolled at the Harrington School of Design in the Fine Arts Building on Michigan Avenue, downtown.

Now my load became even heavier. I had tons of schoolwork, hardly slept anymore, studied, and worked all night. I found out Rod was involved with drugs. I could not get him to talk to me or help him with his struggles at school and with friends. The divorce really affected him emotionally. He was smart, a fast learner, and did not require much preparation for his classes. Having been so busy with hockey, he had not gotten into other sports, so now he had too much time on his hands. I met with Emery, and after some arguing, he decided Rod needed to come to live with him.

Rod needed a father's attention, not mine. So, reluctantly, Rod moved in with his father, who by now also had moved to Lake Bluff and lived within walking distance from us. I felt terrible, for I knew Rod and Emery did not get along at all. I wanted my son to stay, but was worried about drugs, which were so big in those days. I was also worried about his grades so he could make it into a good college. Once he started living with his dad, he was much more supervised and his grades improved.

Opening My First Business

⁓

I left Peterson Interiors and decided to open a shop in Long Grove, a town known for its lovely antique shops. It was full of boutiques, cafés, and restaurants, and people came by busloads to shop, eat, and spend the day. My shop was called Woodhue Interiors, and I sold handcrafted items, accessories for the home, and offered decorating services.

I had lots of items on consignment from craftsmen, like the beautiful tables, clocks, and boxes made from the giant sequoias of California. They were very popular in those days. I also traveled to Mexico and loaded up on many lovely handcrafts, and traveled to West Africa and purchased carvings and huge batiks, macramé, and very unusual and interesting pieces. It was a success! The store's layout and merchandise were lovely.

I also added a little antique photo shop upstairs, on the second level, with the kids in mind. I was hoping they would run the antique photo shop, which was a simple process of a polaroid camera placed inside an old camera that looked authentic. We took pictures of couples or groups who dressed up in the various costumes we provided to make them look Victorian. We had hats, parasols, jackets, dresses and even fake mustaches, which they would put on and then pose for the pictures. Then we used a solution to age the photos, and put them in Victorian frames.

My kids were not as enthusiastic about this photo shop as I was. Cookie got a summer job on the beach, and Rod was never around to come with me to the store. It was a lot of work, but I loved my life, traveling through the wheat fields in the mornings on my way to open my lovely store and spend the day with customers and sell. I had my good friends, Agnes and Clint Nelson, helping when I needed it.

At this time in my life, I met someone significant. "There is the carnal knowledge of the senses that include carnal happiness, and a greater knowledge that comes from intellect and reason." Sometimes it is not easy to connect to the latter. When the senses take over and reason disappears, it's nice to go with the overwhelming sensation, which is unstoppable, it seems. If you need to stop and think and reason, it ruins the moment, and it will never return.

When I first met Lance, it was unlike anything else in my life; sparks began flying, for his touch triggered a whole bodily reaction unfamiliar to me until this point.

We were at opposite sides of the room at a large gathering, and it was like a magnet drawing us together in the crowded room. We looked across the room at each other at the same moment, and I saw a tall blond with a smile that lit up his whole face. He stuck out from the crowd with his height and good looks, athletic build, broad shoulders, and green-blue eyes. I was smitten the moment he appeared next to me and offered me a drink, which I accepted gratefully. We were under a spell, and could not wait to leave the meeting to spend time to get to know each other.

The attraction was so palpable on both sides that we just gave into the moment. Not only did we become lovers but good friends for years to come. The passion never left, although I hurt him deeply when he chose to visit his mother in Tennessee for Christmas instead of staying with me. It was my first Christmas as a divorcee, and I was hurt and angry about his choice. (How silly of me.) I wanted nothing to do with him and would not answer his calls. But when he returned with a brightly wrapped, large package, which contained a fur coat as a peace offering, I forgave him. Our relationship was physical: we could not be together without touching and kissing. I felt powerless in his presence, and so was he in mine.

He owned an impressive home-remodeling business, Kitchen Showcase, in the heart of Kenilworth, a North Shore community. He lived above his shop and showrooms where you could smell freshly sanded wood, the smell of which reminded me of Father's furniture shop back in Hungary. Our lives drifted apart when I moved to the city and started my next business, the day spa, and met Joe, my future husband. I later learned that Lance had contacted aids, sold his business, and moved to Las

Vegas with some friend. We last saw each other at a surprise birthday party that Joe, my new husband, had arranged for me. Lance had lost a lot of weight, but he was still the charmer. He passed away in Las Vegas at the age of fifty-eight.

After a couple of years of store, kids, home, and yard, I also became involved with EST, the Werner Erhard workshop. After I graduated the program, I had Emery and both kids take it also. Then I also studied to become a seminar leader, and began conducting seminars downtown in the evenings. It was time to sell the shop. In no time I had a buyer. I was determined to start a new business called New Dimensions, and had a partner named Snookie from Saint Louis, who was also very active in EST. She and her husband, Lee, would drive from Saint Louis to Chicago for seminars.

Snookie and I looked for and found the perfect place in the center of Deerfield, on the North Shore, where we signed a lease, and we started planning the interior. In the interim, I took a wonderful trip to Machu Picchu, Peru, which was a very special spiritual experience for me. On returning and getting all the new and necessary items in the space, I opened the doors to my new business of body wrapping and tanning. It required long hours six days a week and did not make much money right off, not even enough to cover expenses.

Moving Downtown

≈

hen one day, a lovely woman named Natasha Hoffer walked in the salon, had the treatments, and asked me if I would be willing to relocate downtown. She said she had just the perfect spot for this business, no one else was doing it in the city, and I should consider it. I visited the location—it was on East Delaware Street just behind the Hancock Building and the Water Tower, an excellent location on the Magnificent Mile. For the first time, I seriously considered relocating downtown and moving from far away Lake Bluff.

The shop had previously been a men's salon and now stood empty. It was inside a huge unisex salon that had many operators and stations, specialty hair experts, and a manicurist. One of the owners was an interior designer, and together we planned out my needs. He began work on it right away, adding a shower, a room for the washer and dryer, sinks, and counter space for preparing the wraps. He also designed some very clever fold-up beds so the rooms could be used for both wrapping and resting for the clients, who were required to rest with the wrappings on for at least an hour. They had earphones so they could listen to guided-meditation tapes or soft music. I also added facials, hair removal, and had a tanning bed, which was used a lot. The hair removal was a much desired service for men and women, as were massages. It was the first day spa in downtown Chicago. I even needed a zoning change, which I got in no time from the mayor, Richard Daily.

Before long, I was introduced to the editor of the local paper called *Magnificent Mile*, and he wrote a very nice article to introduce Eva's Body Wrap. People came out of curiosity at first but returned because they loved it. It was a "quiet oasis" in the busy city. Word spread through the building, which was a residential high-rise, as well as through the neighborhood. I hired two people and trained them, and finally moved my own residence from Lake Bluff to the city. My first apartment was a pleasant loft space on Dearborn with a complete health club and pool.

By this time, Cookie was studying at the University of Indiana at Bloomington. She studied accounting at her father's suggestion. Rod was a freshman at the University of Illinois in Champaign studying figure drawing and sculpting, fields in which he was so very talented. I enjoyed living downtown—it had a different vibe—and I rented the house to a family from Lake Forest, who agreed to paint and take care of the gardens instead of paying rent.

Alas, they did not deliver. I felt very lucky when they moved out one night, without ever paying me. I decided to sell the house because it was too much work for me to look after.

Having my business downtown, my hours were cut considerably; I only worked from nine to six five days a week and had weekends free. I became friends with Natasha, whose two daughters worked in the salon as hairdressers.

On weekends, I would visit Natasha and her husband, RM, in Evanston. Together we enjoyed gardening, cooking, and shopping in the suburbs. I was never a city person and loved being close to the earth, therefore gardening was a special hobby.

We partied a lot, even spent nights at the famous Playboy Mansion, and joined a singles group at the Hyatt Hotel once a week. Soon I moved a little closer to the salon, to the Doral on Michigan Avenue, which was a comfortable walk every morning. The building, again, had a full health club with state-of-the-art equipment, a beautiful large swimming pool, a sauna, and a dressing area.

The Lyric Opera of Chicago housed all their singers and conductors at the Doral, and using the club was the best way to build my business. Before long, I had Sir George Solti as a client. Tatiana Troianos, the soprano, I met in the steam room, and we became friends, as did so did many of the great opera singers and conductors who stayed at the Doral.

Sir Solti was the conductor of the Chicago Symphony, and lived in the Mayfair Hotel, where I visited him and his wife, Valerie. He even got me tickets when I asked. Later on, when Joe and I visited London, we watched him conduct at Carnegie Hall, from their box. He was a very special and great man. Since conducting opera requires always looking up at the stage, he developed some serious muscle problems as he grew older, including having difficulty moving his neck. He required special massage and would have only me work on him, which was an honor. A funny incident happened years later when we were at Carnegie Hall in the Solti's box as guests. Joe ordered champagne, and right at the moment when there was a pause in the music, Joe shifted in his seat and tipped the tray with the flutes, creating a commotion. Sir Solti immediately looked up, letting us know he was aware of who made the shattering noise, which made me want to hide!

Meeting Joe Saunders

Again, the best part of moving my business to the city was meeting my future husband, Joe Saunders. He spent a lot of time in Chicago on business and had time on his hands to get pampered, so he often came to the salon for haircuts, body wraps, facials, and massages. He would ask me to have dinner with him so he would not be eating alone. I enjoyed his company. He was the perfect gentleman and never abused our relationship. We had to keep it a straight friendship since he was a married man. We even went to concerts or plays, very casually.

He was president of his organization and would stay in Chicago once every few months. We had known each other for six years, when one day, he called me with the sad news: he had lost his wife in a single car accident very near their home after he had returned from an around the world trip. He was devastated, and I tried to console him the best I could. He told me he was going back to Europe to get some distance and to heal. Weeks later I received a call from him. He was in Ireland with his best friends, Bob and Pat Foot, who lived in Howth, near Dublin. They enjoyed each other's company and were able to help him recover from his loss. Pat suggested that Joe call me and ask me to meet up in the Caribbean. One busy day, he called me from Ireland, and I could tell he had been drinking. He sounded very jolly, and asked me to meet him in Martinique. I assumed he was under the influence and would forget about it the next day. However, a few days later, I received tickets by FedEx, and knew it was for real. I was excited; I started planning and packing, and before long it was time to go!

Martinique With Joe, 1987

It was very early in the morning, and a big snowstorm was raging as happens only in Chicago. I now lived at Outer Drive East, a lovely condominium overlooking the drive, Grant Park, and the skyline. Trying to get a cab when the line was twelve-people long was close to hopeless. Fortunately, I found another person in the long line who was also going to the airport, and the two of us prayed the whole way that we would make our flights. The snow kept falling, roads were not yet cleared, and driving was hazardous under these conditions.

We finally arrived at O'Hare Airport on time! I rushed to the gate and was on my way to meet Joe, now a widower and a possible partner. I was so excited because this was my first trip with Joe. I did not know what to expect, but I always had a curious and adventurous spirit, which helped.

When I arrived, a very happy Joe was waiting at the gate with a bouquet of roses and a big smile! I embraced him, and our vacation began by exploring the island of lovely Martinique. It has a Dutch and a French side, each very different, and we stayed on the French side of the island, adjacent to the nude beach. After driving around and checking out both sides, I suggested he get a hat since he was so fair and the tropical sun so intense.

We undressed for the beach—nude of course. It was so delightful to be in the warm gentle waves in the middle of winter, enjoying the sunshine and just floating and body surfing. By the end of the day, we were sunburned in places never exposed to the sun. As I got in the shower, I was hurting and so was Joe, both of us red like well-done lobsters. We rushed to get some aloe, gently apply it all over to soothe the burn, and drank flutes of champagne.

Then we dressed for dinner and enjoyed the most exquisite meal I have ever tasted. I will never forget it, down to the amazing coconut flambé, which I was never able to duplicate. It was so romantic. We were served the finest French wines and the most amazing food. Joe really knew how to spoil a woman, and he spoiled me! We stopped in at the casino, but we were not interested in gambling, just people watching and some after dinner drinks. I was sure I was in heaven. He wanted to totally sweep me off my feet, and nearly managed.

The next day he had a little surprise for me. We were going to fly over to Saint Barth to visit his friends from Paris. After the amazing flight, we had a breathtaking landing just over the mountains between the sea and the hills, a very narrow landing strip. We arrived at their home and were soon sitting around the pool, clothing optional. Jacqueline was naked, smoking, and offering me champagne. I have never been a prude, but having a very curvaceous woman sitting nude and so comfortable made me a little ill at ease with my shorts and T-shirt on. Marcel, the husband, wore the tiniest little triangles to barely cover the necessities.

Having enjoyed the visit and the lovely Saint Barths, it was time to fly back to our island. The next day, Joe decided to take a hydrofoil to Saba, the volcanic island known for diving and snorkeling. It had no beaches, just volcanic rocks popping out of the ocean, creating a tropical paradise with fruit trees unknown to us. There were fragrant flowers, and orchids the size of footballs in every color and shape. It was a magical place.

There were even exotic birds like toucans and wild parrots everywhere, and the hydrofoil on which we traveled was an experience in itself.

I was familiar with Martinique, having spent a fun vacation there with Emery and the children at Club Med. I had even taught yoga there when they temporarily lost their yoga teacher and I took over. This had been many years earlier; the children had learned some French at their daily lessons and so were totally free to roam in their designated facility with other children from all over the world. That was a very different experience.

Joe and I really bonded in Martinique, sampling the many restaurants, enjoying remarkable wines, feasting on food meant for the gods. Still, after ten unforgettable days, it was time to return to our busy lives.

I received a CD player with many CDs of my favorite music—hard to find in those days—and I packed them in my checked bag. When I arrived back at O'Hare, my bag was nowhere to be found. I made a claim and eventually it showed up, minus the CD player and the CDs. I was so disappointed, but no one was willing to be responsible.

Joe began to spend more time in Chicago visiting me, and we started going to concerts, the opera, and the theater. At one point, I invited him to a concert by the great Hungarian concert pianist, Andras Kocsis. We loved the beautiful selections he played at Orchestra Hall, and we were asked over to a friend's house for a little reception. It was the first time Joe saw me interact in a social setting, and I guess he liked what he saw. I yelled at the artist that he needed to get his hair cut—it was long and uncared for—and that he must have it done first thing in the morning. I then presented Andras Kocsis with a business card to the salon. That was the night Joe proposed to me.

The Proposal, 1987

≈

When we walked home from the reception, I asked Joe up to see my place. I lived on the thirty-ninth floor of this amazing building, with the balcony overlooking Grant Park and Lake Michigan. It had breathtaking views. There he very ceremoniously got down on his knees and asked me to marry him, which I accepted without hesitation, and it was the best move I ever made. We had an ideal life together for twenty-eight years, double the time I was married to Emery, my first husband.

We started planning our life together. I did not know what it was going to look like, but I knew I had a winner. Joe was smart, intelligent, well-read, and well-bred, with continental manners and an inquisitive mind. Everything interested him. He loved to travel, and we both loved nature, not city living. He started his own business with his father in 1944, just after the war ended. He had served in WWII but never saw action. By the time he went through basic training and was shipped out to the Philippines, the war had ended and he was an MP. He said it had been a great adventure and learning experience, and he wanted to keep traveling. His father needed him, however, so he rushed back home to comply. The first printing press arrived the same day he returned. He even married a lady who, fortunately, had a car, which was needed for the new business.

Joe and his parents worked hard to make their new invention of metal clipboards and A-holders for deliverymen and airlines into a viable business. His father's idea came from watching an oil deliveryman dip his oil stick into a tank, then try to write the amount on a slip of paper, which needed to be signed. Harry, Joe's dad, decided there has to be an easier way. He came up with the design for the clipboard attached to a box, all made out of aluminum for durability, creating a writing surface and a place to store the receipts. Manufacturing and marketing this new invention was hard work, but with persistence it caught on. Now Louise, Joe's wife, joined the workforce at Saunders Manufacturing. Although she was a home economics teacher, another pair of hands came in very handy.

The business involved a lot of time on the road, traveling to trade shows to introduce these new products: A-holders and clipboards of all sizes and materials. Saunders Manufacturing got into some stationery stores. It took years, but eventually the product got recognition and full distribution. In those days, there were thousands of stationary stores all over the country. By the time Joe sold the company in 2008, there were only a handful left. The big-box stores had taken over and forced the mom-and-pop operations out of business. The company now had to deal with price control, Chinese imports, and only a handful of businesses, like Staples, Office Max, Cosco, and Walmart.

Rod and Betsy Get Married

≈

It was around this time that Rod met Betsy Armstrong at the University of Illinois. I loved her the moment we met.

She was a pretty blond with the biggest blue eyes and a great personality; she was a real charmer. Together they decided to take a semester in Vienna, Austria, where they would live with Mother. They learned quickly what a difference there is in education between the two countries, and how revered the professors are in Europe, though much less accessible. They enjoyed living with Mother, traveling on weekends to visit nearby countries, seeing museums, and learning so much. Betsy was a delightful, pretty girl, very friendly and outgoing. It was no surprise Rod fell in love with her.

When they returned, they told us, "We are getting married," and as much as we tried to oppose, there was no stopping them. They were so determined, both of them only twenty-one and still in school. They had a lovely wedding ceremony and reception in Rockford, Illinois, and began life on their own. Not long after, Betsy got pregnant—when they came to visit us, she was already showing a little bump. When she delivered a lovely baby boy, Maxwell Armstrong, Rod was there and helped with the delivery. They were the cutest proud parents. I was allowed in after the baby was cleaned up, and was delighted to hold him. It was overwhelming to see these young parents, still children in my eyes, having their own child.

Max was the first grandchild on both sides, the celebrated first grandbaby in the family, whom everyone loved. He grew fast, and was a happy baby. In the summer of 1991, when they came to visit us in Maine, Betsy was already very pregnant with her second child. Their car was very old, so we decided to replace it with a new SUV, providing safe transportation to this growing family. Joy was born in January, and I rushed to be there to take care of Max while the parents were busy with the new baby. At this time, Rod had already finished with his master's degree in fine arts and was teaching at the Art Institute of Chicago, a great achievement! Unfortunately, the pay was not enough to support a family, and after looking around, he took a position in Kalamazoo, Michigan as the director of their art institute. He also received a commission from Japan for one of his sculptures, which helped financially. They rented a lovely home in the country and moved to Kalamazoo.

When Max turned three and a half, he was diagnosed with autism. I immediately took a trip to be with them. At first I was in denial, not wanting to believe this devastating news. After doing a lot of reading and research, I had to accept the facts. I spent some time with the two little ones while Betsy visited her mother in Rockford—she was undergoing chemo for breast cancer. Their life now was a struggle, mostly because Betsy took many trips to be with her sick mother while Rod was working and taking care of the kids. I tried to help as much as I could, but I had my own life with my very special husband and his business, where I had been voted onto the board of directors and had new responsibilities.

I also read and learned all I could about autism, and found a place in Toronto, called The Hearing Center, where they worked with autistic children. The program ran for three weeks and then took a week off followed by two more weeks. It consisted of listening by earphone to familiar sounds, like Mozart music, and slowly removing some of the high-pitched notes; it was designed to increase the skill of listening. This really helped Max, and his language and vocabulary improved. The first time we all went—Betsy, Joy, Max, and I—we had fun. The second time, Betsy chose to stay home with Joy. We had plenty of time to explore this wonderful Canadian city and it's many ethnic neighborhoods. All this happened after Joe and I were already married.

Meeting the Family

〜

After we became engaged, Joe took me to his favorite cousins in Maryland to introduce me as his fiancé. He was close to them, more like siblings since he was an only child. We stayed with Judy and her husband, Bob, in Crownsville on the farm, which was still the original Saunders farm owned by Joe's Uncle Willard and his wife, Eleanor. The only house built on the property was the original farmhouse in which the family had lived after many years of travel (they had been stationed in several places since Willard was an admiral in the navy). After Willard passed away, daughter Judy and her husband, Bob, build their home on the property to be near her mother, Eleanor. Judy's twin sister lived in Falls Church, Virginia, where she worked as a travel agent. She frequently came to the farm on weekends and holidays to be with family. Both Bob and Judy worked at National Geographic, which was where they had met. They enjoyed gardening and had a beautiful home on the Severance River, which is where the farm was located.

Next, Judy's brother, Wesley, and his wife, Ann, decided to build a beautiful home with a pool right there on the river. In the following years, they developed the farm and sold homesites of an acre or more. Before long, the farm was gone, and a new suburb had been created.

I enjoyed meeting the family, and they were very welcoming to me as part of the Saunders family. We picked apples, made tons of applesauce, and had a lovely reception so I could meet many of their friends. By the time we left, I really felt I belonged! We kept our friendship over the years, and were invited to sister Patient's wedding in the beautiful gardens at the farm. Unfortunately, the marriage did not last. She wanted to keep working after she married, but the senator would not allow it, so it ended fast.

Next, Joe arranged a little reception for me to see my future home in rural Readfield, Maine. We arrived in Portland and kept driving north toward our home. I saw mostly pine trees and some open land, but once we arrived on the long, curving drive leading up to the house, I knew I was home! The place was right on the water, with a deck actually hanging over the waves. I loved what I saw and knew, with a little change to the decor, I would be very satisfied and comfortable here.

Everyone was very welcoming, even Joe's children, Harry and Peggy. My father-in-law, Harry Sr., was especially warm and pleasant. I met all the people important in the company, including Joe's secretary, Betty, who was delighted to see him remarry. I loved getting to know the people in Joe's life. Both his son and daughter worked at the company as well as his daughter-in-law, Donna. Harry Jr., had married her and adopted her two young children, which made his parents very happy—they now had grandchildren!

I still had my business, The Body Wrap, in Chicago, and it was hard for me to part with, for I loved the business, my clients, and my lifestyle. However, Joe was anxious for me to move to Maine. We talked on the phone for hours daily; he began to paint with acrylic in the evenings, as he did not know what else to do. We visited each other on weekends, and he waited patiently for me to finally make the move. He came more often than I, but eventually, I gave the business to my sister, Betty, who needed a job at the time. I had decided it would be a better life for her than working for someone else. The only problem was the long commute, for she lived in a far western suburb called Glendale Heights. She did enjoy the business, creating her own clients and losing my old ones.

She was also raising her granddaughter, Alexis, which made travel to the city even more difficult, for she wanted to be there for her as much as possible. Betty met the challenge and was now owner and operator of The Body Wrap.

The Wedding, 1987

~

Joe wanted to have a wonderful celebration to show the world how happy he was. A big wedding meant lots of planning. I began shopping for a wedding gown and found it in Dallas at a Neiman Marcus store. It was a simple off-white satin gown with a simple hat and veil, one I could wear again for a formal occasion. Our favorite hotel in Chicago was the Water Tower Hyatt, admired for its location and the first class restaurant and service it offered. (Sadly, it no longer exists, having been replaced by a much larger hotel.) Joe booked the bright ballroom, and we invited around a hundred guests. This included all the company management from Maine; our lawyer, Sumner Lipman, and his wife, Dawn; our European manager, Theo Van Der Mars, his secretary, Bep, and her husband, Emil Tamenga; Joe's family; many of my friends and coworkers; my sisters and their families; and cousins from as far away as Budapest and Montreal.

Since most of our guests and family were from out of town, we had a huge rehearsal dinner with all of the out-of-town guests invited, and even a breakfast the following morning before we left for our honeymoon. It was a truly international crowd! They were served amazing wines, champagne, and food. My bouquet was painted lilies, the fragrant variety, which were my favorite flowers. For me, it was a storybook wedding, and made up for the first not-so-great one. Joe was the happiest groom I could ever have had. I felt very loved and treasured. We so enjoyed each other's company.

The Honeymoon

≈

It began in Los Angeles, California. We had flown there first class, stayed at the luxurious Beverly Hills Hotel, and spent some time exploring the city. We visited the La Brea Tar Pits, shopped on Rodeo Drive, saw landmark buildings and famous stars' homes, and enjoyed our very plush hotel with it's fabulous history.

Then it was time to fly on to Hawaii. Again, we traveled first class. Our first stop was Luau, the garden island with so many various climates and altitudes that it was considered a natural wonder. Just the drive to our resort was captivating, and once there, we found a picture-perfect place, with a little shuttle running from the entrance to the rooms, the various pools, and the lounges. It was a tropical paradise with exotic flowers everywhere! We spent a few lovely days here, driving around to see the hills and valleys of this magical island. We drove from the highest peak to the cool valleys, which were covered with moss from the constant moisture. After Luau, we flew on to the big island, Honolulu. I was reading *Hawaii* by James Michener, which gave me a deeper appreciation of these islands, the history, and its people. As secluded as Luau was, Honolulu was a bustling, busy city with so much to see and do. We visited museums, the active volcano, and dined at some good restaurants, among them Nick's Fishmarket restaurant, his original one. Nick had also opened a restaurant with the same name in downtown Chicago, which is where I knew him from. Nick was a friend of a friend and client, and his restaurant had the best seafood flown in fresh daily to town.

We stayed on the beach where we could swim and snorkel, and took long walks to watch skillful surfers glide over huge waves, disappearing and reappearing as they would speed along the surface of the water.

We admired the beauty of Waikiki Beach, and took a glass-bottomed boat to see the colorful creatures beneath the surface. After spending a week in these magical islands, I never wanted to leave. To me it seemed "we had arrived," but there was a lot more to come.

The next flight to New Zealand was a long one, and we had to deplane and fly on to Melbourne for a meeting with a business client/friend of Joe's. He invited us to his lovely home and showed us around the area, and he took us to dinner at his elegant club, one of many in Melbourne. I saw my first live kangaroo there, in their backyard!

There were many strange, unusual animals, like enormous fruit bats, which hung upside down in the trees! It so happened that the Australian Open was on, and our hotel windows looked right down onto the Rod Laver Arena. It was even more exciting to be able to watch some of the tennis greats play.

After inspecting as much as we could in this very British and charming city, we flew on to Sidney. What a contrast! Sidney is a very modern and cosmopolitan city with so much to offer. Again, we met some business friends of Joe's. It was always nice to have a local guide who pointed out many things of interest to us. We also explored on our own, finding some irresistible restaurants, shops, and street markets. We were even able to get tickets to the famous Sydney Opera House, where we saw an unforgettable production of *The Pearl Fishers* by Georges Bizet. After seeing the important sights and walking our legs off, it was time to get out into nature.

We next flew to Fiji where we were transported to an exceptional resort. Here all the dining was outdoors, and even the bathrooms were both inside and out. It was a new paradise found, and it had the most amazing flowers and birds. We snorkeled on a little island where they had just finished filming *Castaway* with Tom Hanks. This lovely island had gained celebrity status because of the filming and the Hollywood stars.

The highlight for me was visiting a native village by dugout canoe. Here the Aboriginal Australians still lived in a very primitive way, just as they had for centuries. They showed us around by canoe and served us a lovely meal where we were seated on the ground, eating from banana leaves by hand. I will never forget this simple pleasure, the warm welcome we received, and the fragrant flowers we were given by the children.

Our trip was still not over. We continued following the sun to Europe, where we stopped to visit our headquarters in the Netherlands. Then we stopped to see Mother in Vienna before returning to Chicago.

Surprise Birthday Bash, 1988

≈

While still living in Chicago, now married and commuting, Joe arranged for a surprise birthday party for me at a Hungarian delicatessen and restaurant on Belmont Avenue called Szekrenyi. The owner was a wine importer and had an extensive selection of European wines There was a bakery upstairs and a lovely wine cellar and restaurant downstairs. With Betty's and Natasha's help, Joe was able to invite all my close friends and family and completely surprise me. I had never had a surprise party thrown for me, and I was totally overcome emotionally. To see so many of my friends and family under one roof and to be able to celebrate with them—I was ecstatic!

Life in Maine

≈

Giving my business to Betty allowed me to make the move, say goodbye to my lovely apartment in Chicago, and relocate to Readfield, Maine, my new home—my new life! I wanted to keep just a few special pieces that I could not leave behind. I arrived in Maine, and Joe was delighted. He immediately gave me permission to make any changes I wanted to the house so it would feel like home.

Joe had originally purchased the property as a summer cottage, and it had a history from prohibition days. It had been a rum-running operation, where you could quickly slide down a pole from the top floor to the water and get out without being detected.

After he bought it, the house was lifted up, and a full basement was put under it. Next, full insulation was added so that it was now heated centrally instead of with just a wood-burning fire. Only then did Joe move his family in. All this renovation happened between 1969 and 1971. It was an amazingly private property, where we could swim naked.

I began my renovation at the top, starting with the bedrooms, adding extra closet space, a new skylight, and an enlarged bathroom. I even turned one bedroom into my exercise room. Joe had collected amazing paintings from local artists such as Alex Katz and Neil Welliver. He had so many paintings that the house was like an art gallery. The living room was two stories high with a balcony all around, and the walls were filled with art. It had a central staircase, beautifully crafted from walnut. The river-stone fireplace was also two stories high, with an oversized mantel made out of a solid piece of wood that was the focal point.

We soon started shopping for furniture, and Joe agreed with most things I wanted. I still had my designer privileges at the Merchandise Mart showrooms, so I purchased some lovely pieces and combined them with the existing antiques from the house, creating an eclectic decor; Joe loved the result. We discussed everything first, but I was pretty clear on most ideas, such as making the main entrance to the house central. Now, when you entered the house, you could immediately see the water. It made a huge difference to the whole place. It did not bother him that we had to hire an architect to redesign the rooflines. He wanted me to be happy, and I was.

Once I settled into my life in Maine, I learned to windsurf. I got a board and started to surf on our lake, which occasionally had some serious waves, mostly when the weather cooled. I would be out for hours in the wind and would get very cold, so Joe installed a hot tub on the deck, which was a lifesaver for me. He also converted the guest-bathroom shower into a steam bath, which we used mostly in winter after cross-country skiing across the lake. It was heavenly!

Every time we returned from a trip, more work had been completed on the house, which was a pleasant surprise. After I was finished redecorating the whole house, we traveled a lot, going to various printing industry and stationary shows from Chicago to Amsterdam to Frankfurt. Every time we were in Europe, we made a trip to Vienna to see Mother.

Now that the house was to my liking, I began to teach yoga at the local YMCA in Augusta, and Joe came along and walked the hour while I was teaching my class. He had many friends to converse with who also walked with him. After our exercise, we would jump into the lake in the summer months, followed by a breakfast of oatmeal and fresh fruit on the deck, over the water. If it was an especially calm day, I would ask Joe to get the boat started, and he would pull me waterskiing, which was another fun watersport I loved. He often did this before he went to the office, for he always put me first no matter what I asked.

Life was so enjoyable in Maine. We had many friends to visit, and many came to visit us from Chicago, Holland, and even from Japan. We also traveled a great deal in between visitors. I enjoyed entertaining and was fond of giving parties, such as the fundraisers we had annually for the theater at Monmouth—the Shakespearean theater where I became a board member in order to actively support this fabulous attraction in summer months. We loved meeting so many of the elite actors who came from Boston, New York, and California to spend their summer vacation in rural Maine while performing on stage.

I even rekindled my relationship with a friend from Vienna, who had spent several years with the International Theater in Vienna and came to Monmouth one summer. More recently, she directed a show in St. Petersburg, Florida and invited us to see the show at the American Theater.

My grandchildren grew up on Shakespeare plays, watching them all summer as they visited. Life was good. Joe delighted in all our activities. We made some short driving trips to Montreal to visit my cousin Nelly, and they also came to visit us. There was always a Hungarian picnic at the end of summer with some good food and wines from Hungary. This picnic attracted the Hungarian population from as far away as New Hampshire and Massachusetts! My friend Christine was the organizer of the community. She ran a little bakery/café in Augusta, and enjoyed getting together to practice her Hungarian. At these events, we had music and sometimes entertainment or maybe just a few of us dancing. The picnics signaled the end of summer. It was time to get ready for the most colorful season—autumn—when all the leaves became red, orange, and purple, and created a new beauty. People would drive up from all parts to see the trees, especially the maples, take on a beauty of their own!

This time of year, the waves were great for windsurfing, though I needed to pull on a wetsuit for all watersports. How nice it was to have the hot tub to warm up in! I also worked very hard on a little vegetable/herb garden, but the soil was tough clay, and after all the effort, the deer and rabbits enjoyed most of it. I did have lovely window boxes of geraniums on the lower windows and some colorful hanging baskets of many different flowers to add life. I planted a dozen hydrangeas around the tennis court, which bloomed so beautifully, like big snowballs. Once the frost set in, they turned pink and purple, and I would cut some to decorate the house. I always had fresh flowers to cut for the table. I so enjoyed living in Maine, watching a moose or a deer wander by, and on occasion even a bear! Traveling the world was nice, but I was always happy to return to our beautiful home.

Our first trip to visit Mother was before we were married; I wanted to introduce Joe to her. He did not want to sleep with me in my mother's house, so we stayed at the Imperial Hotel. It was more like an early honeymoon. My mother and Joe really liked each other, even with the language difficulty. Her English was from high school, while English was the only language Joe spoke, but he made an effort to learn words in both German and Hungarian so he could communicate.

We took many little trips with Mother, at first just in Austria, in her little Fiat, to get to know the country. Later we extended our travels to include Italy, Germany, Luxemburg, Hungary, and even spent an exotic winter in Egypt, which Mother had always wanted to visit. Joe was a big guy, and for longer trips, the Fiat was just too uncomfortable; we needed to rent a larger car.

We visited Uncle Nandi, Mother's only brother, in Munich, and friends and family still living in Hungary. We all enjoyed shopping for art and unusual pieces of antiques wherever we visited, and acquired quite a collection. Some pieces we left in Vienna, some we shipped or carried back to Maine. I still have some of the special pieces we acquired on these wondrous trips, reminders of happy times with Mother. They fill my walls today. Joe's motto was "The best gift you can give a loved one is happy memories," and he lived by it!

Young Visitors From Europe, 1991

We met a young man in Vienna named Christian, who had designed some very interesting purses and bags from aluminum and rubber and was selling them at the local art-museum shop. We liked him, and Joe invited him to come and work at Saunders for a summer, and to get his bags made here for the company. He came for a few months and made some beautiful bags, attaché cases, and even architect's tubes. They were lovely, and we could not wait to introduce them to the market. However, we soon found out these items had a totally different distribution channel than the ones we used for our products. It was unfortunate, for so much time and money had been invested and very few sold. We had an attic filled with thousands of these lovely products and could not sell them. They ended up in a resale distributors warehouse.

Besides Christian from Vienna, we also hosted the son of a business associate from Belgium, named Stephan; they both stayed in the guesthouse on the property. In addition, there was Angela, the daughter of another business associate from Germany, who stayed with us in the house. They all spent the summer vacation with us, learning and practicing English. I had a playful time with them! Stephan was the youngest, at seventeen; Angela was eighteen, and Christian was in his twenties. It was fun to play with them and teach and entertain them. We spent time gardening, playing tennis, swimming, boating, waterskiing, and windsurfing. We cooked and baked and grilled a lot, and took some trips to Arcadia National Park and to Boston.

We also met some students from overseas who worked at the nearby camps as counselors, and we had them over for meals and fun on their days off. Vicky was Hungarian; Erica was Czech; and Daria was Polish; they were students working in these prestigious camps. We entertained the young, the old, and everyone in between, and had so much fun doing it. Later, when we were in London, we visited Daria, who had married a British chap. And when we were in Budapest, we met with Vicky Varga, who had married and was expecting a baby. These were such special moments in life—making special friends.

A European Adventure, 1994

≈

Our trip began in New York on May 8th. We enjoyed a spring visit to the Big Apple with Theo van der Mars. I also celebrated my birthday with my daughter, Charmaine, and her college roommate, Dawn—just the three of us girls. The next day the "boys" took me for a fabulous lunch at the Park Lane Hotel, after which we left for Europe.

We spent two lovely spring days in Amsterdam, where we saw Bep Tammanga's art show in an unusual setting, and we could not help but purchase some pieces to ship home. She has come a long way as a watercolor painter!

On May 16th, we arrived in Vienna, where Mother anxiously awaited us. After a few days of preparation, we departed for Italy, this time in a full-sized, air-conditioned rental car. It was the day Jackie Onassis died. When we arrived in Venice, which was Mom's favorite city in Italy, it was raining slightly, and we headed for the hotel San Marco. It was difficult to find a porter in the drizzle, but after we located one, we took a water taxi to the hotel, which gave us our first glimpses of this amazing city on the canals. We were treated to a magical rainbow that surrounded all of Venice—a good omen! It was a perfect photo opportunity, but my camera was packed.

Our first stop was the Basilica di San Marco, followed by the Palazzo Ducale, Pont dei Sospiri, Ponte di Rialto, and Murano and the glass factory, and then a gondola ride. We listened to great music in the piazza and had some Italian food and wine. On Sunday morning, we were treated to a marvelous spectacle, for the once-a-year regatta was on! All the gondoliers were dressed in their most colorful costumes as they raced each other down the canals.

Our next stop was Verona (we were unable to get accommodations in Florence due to the holiday weekend). We stayed in a lovely hotel halfway between Verona and Lago di Garda, where the Italian Open was taking place. We liked watching some great tennis. Our hotel was a 14th century, converted monastery, luxuriously refurbished, with an amazing restaurant that served meals fit for a king! The service was extraordinary; it took us a half-day to find it, but it was well worth the effort. It was called Villa Quaranta Park Hotel in Ospeneletto di Pescantina.

The next morning, our concierge tried to make reservations for Florence, which took a while; they finally booked us into the Villa Belvedere, just two kilometers out of the city. It was located up on a hill overlooking all of Florence, and had a pool and flower gardens in full bloom. The rooms were spacious, with balconies. I ran out for a swim before we went on the city tour, where we learned more about our beautiful surroundings and their past. Our guide was in love with Michelangelo, who had made the city famous. He had so much information and shared it so enthusiastically that he'd lost his voice by the end. We saw the Duomo, the Baptistery, the great Uffizi Palace, and the Boboli Gardens.

We took a ride on Via Michelangelo, where you could get the best overview of the city. We also visited the Museo del Duomo, where we saw the Pieta. The following day, we toured the Archeological Museum and then the Capelle di Medici, which had been converted by Michelangelo and was filled with his sculptures. It was overwhelming! We next went to the churches of St. Lorenzo and St. Marco, and to Pont Vecchio, where we purchased some gold souvenirs, had some Italian ice, and just took in the excitement of this fun and art-filled town.

We dropped Mother at the hotel to rest, and went back to the city at night, when it takes on a new character. We walked and walked, covering the whole city with its many shops. There were little cafés and piazzas, with policemen on every corner so you felt safe. On May 26th, we said our goodbye to Florence and stopped in Sienna on the way to Rome. It is the second most interesting spot in Tuscany. Campo, the huge fan-shaped piazza, alone is worth the trip. The Palazzo Publico, from the 13th century, had a 335-meter tower with great views from the top. The cathedral museum contained some original frescoes from the 14th century by Lorenzetti. The 14th-century Palazzo Buonsignori had a large collection of Sienese art from the

14th through the 17th centuries. It was a delight to wander through as many of the medieval streets as you could, stopping at the churches, each a museum in itself. The ancient cobblestones were worn out from centuries of traffic.

After an alfresco lunch, we left for Rome via SS2, driving along the shores of Lago di Bolsena, where the town of Capodimonte is located, famous for its unique porcelain. There is a certain turn along SS2 where you can get a dramatic glimpse of the medieval town of Orvieto, located high above the road on top of the mountain, sitting more like a monument than a vital town. It was worth the extra time to take this route! We arrived in the eternal city of Rome around four in the afternoon. Traffic was overwhelming, with scooters, motorcycles, and cars of all sizes racing in and around the very narrow streets, which were not meant for automobiles. (Cars are forbidden in the inner city, within the walls, and this is enforced.) It took us over two hours to get to our hotel, which was only nineteen kilometers from the center. We chose to stay here because of the lovely pool, but as it turned out, it was not open until the day we left, June 1st.

We immediately signed up for the city tour where they picked you up and returned you to the hotel. The first day, a taxi came to collect us, and the driver really had to hustle to get us there on time! Appian Line Tours was good, with knowledgeable guides. It was well organized and kept as close to schedule as traffic allowed in Rome. We saw the Trevi Fountain, the Pantheon, Piazza Navona, and St. Peter's Basilica. Then we enjoyed a great lunch after which we moved on to the Capital, the Colosseum, the Roman Forum, the basilica of St. Paul, and the church of St. Peter in Chains, which contains Michelangelo's "Moses." Most of the tour was walking, so we were exhausted by the time we were dropped off at the hotel. The next morning, our tour began at eight in the morning and took us to the Vatican Museum and it's crowning glory, the Sistine Chapel. We returned to St. Peter's for a second look and wandered around. Then we arrived at the Piazza dell'Esquilino, one of the most colorful neighborhoods of Rome. Mother and I even did some shopping for Italian, designer clothing, which was a bargain there. We stopped for a well-deserved drink, and picked out a great looking trattoria for an alfresco dinner. What a day this had been! We even walked around to check out the nightlife. My favorite activity in a new city is to find a good spot to people watch, and we had certainly found the best!

On Sunday morning, we headed south toward our next destination, Sorrento. Even the name is romantic. We soon realized Sunday was not a good day to travel by car, but it was too late. We arrived at this lovely property just in time for lunch under the fragrant lemon trees. Sorrento is the home of Limoncello, the liquor made from lemons. It was the Sorrento Palace Hotel, with large but cozy rooms, terraces, and a breathtaking view of the Bay of Naples and Capri. Mount Vesuvius was ever lurking in the background, a cone shaped threat. The resort had one of the most interesting pools I had ever seen; it was on six levels, all connected by slides. We spent the afternoon swimming, sunning, and sliding through the lovely gardens filled with flowers, butterflies, and the fragrance of lemon blossoms. The trees were laden with fruit, and colorful birds were singing their songs. Mother declared she had arrived in paradise. Both food and service were meticulous, and we indulged ourselves in every moment of our three-day stay. For dinner, we ventured into town to a local favorite, according to our concierge. It was a tiny trattoria tucked into a very narrow street, with truly local Neapolitan specialties, including wine from Vesuvio. The romance and charm of this little town is hard to convey with words. With it's amazing setting and a mild subtropical climate, it was a reminder of days gone by. As you walked the streets so narrow, you could touch walls on both sides. Romantic, colorful, Mediterranean architecture abounded, with whitewashed facades, bright amber-tiled roofs, and many charming balconies dripping with bougainvillea and oleander in every color. The streets were cobblestone, with many stairs that were just wide enough for a person to pass. There was a dizzying fragrance in the air, music that came from passing boats, and sometimes a single guitar playing …

We took a hydrofoil to the nearby Isle of Capri, and spent an unforgettable day there. We walked, took many pictures, and just absorbed the beauty of the island with its 360-degree views. Of course, we had to find a little souvenir to take with us! At the end of the day, we took a slow boat back to Sorrento, and I was ready for a cool swim in the pool, for it has been a hot day. Again we went into town after dark, listened to music, stopped for some Italian ice, and just feasted our eyes on these ancient streets and the many happy, smiling faces! We had one last day to spend in this "little bit of heaven on earth" before driving further south.

Next destination was Paestum, Campania, to see what remained of this once flourishing center. Besides the walls, which once surrounded this great city, we saw the basilica, the Temple of Neptune, and the Temple of Ceres, all of which were in remarkable states of preservation even though they had been abandoned in the 9th century. The museum was the best surprise because of the tomb paintings, which were a great example of Greek funerary mural paintings. We especially liked the painting of the diver.

Now it was time to start back north along the Amalfi Coast, which was the highlight of this portion of the trip. Joe wanted to drive it with the sun behind us for best visibility and photography. We stopped for pictures and a short coffee break halfway. Once we arrived in Positano, we stayed for the night. I adored the Moorish houses clinging to the cliffs high above the waters. The town falls almost vertically into the sea. Our hotel was charming, directly above the beach, Hotel L'Ancora, it's balconies opening to magnificent views. Dinner was served on the terrace, which was covered with flowers, the ever-present Isle of Capri still visible in the distance. One could just sit on this lovely flower-covered balcony and watch the busy fishing village below or even the beach with its swimmers. You could watch little boats coming and going as they deposited noisy tourists, or simply catch the ocean breezes, all without moving. You could also choose to climb the hundreds of stairs going up and down these vertical streets in every direction.

We started back north through Naples to the ruins of Cumae. Since we traveled along the coast, we drove through the town of Pozzuoli, Sophia Loren's birthplace, which had a well-preserved amphitheater called Flavio. Just down the road we found Cumae, with its mysterious past. It is so far off the beaten path that very few tourists venture here. However, it was wonderful to see the Solfatara volcano and the Phlegraean Fields. These most unusual natural phenomena have puzzled spectators since ancient times. Cumae's most interesting site is the "Dromos," the cave of the Sibyl, which was a sacred place that only the priests could enter. The town also encompasses the Temple of Apollo, the "Sacred Way," the Christian basilica, the grotto of peace, and Averno Lake.

Almost no other souls were at any of these deserted sites, which made it even more special.

It was time to drive back north toward Rome, with our destination being the town of Baschi, Umbria. Upon arriving at Villa Bellago, which was highly recommended by Fodor, we had to go for a swim to cool off in the Olympic-size pool. It was a perfect location on Lago di Corbara, and we anticipated exploring Umbria's medieval towns, the first being Todi and then Spoletto. The drive alone was incredible, and the little towns were most fascinating. We walked for hours (I don't even know how Mom could keep up with us), for there was so much to see. Then we drove to Orvieto to explore and to try some of its famous wines. Orvieto's glorious Gothic style Duomo was started in the 12th century by Arnolfo di Cambio, the architect of both the Duomo and Palazzo Vecchio in Florence. Mother was amazing, doing so much walking at her age. She just kept going, even when I knew she had to be exhausted. The three of us enjoyed another night at Villa Bellago, took another swim in the cold pool, and drove off to Assisi and Perugia.

It was a lovely, leisurely drive through a countryside that was bursting in spring glory. It was filled with colorful wild flowers and had grape vines draped all over the hillsides.

We drove past many olive groves, peach and apricot orchards, and endless sunflower fields, their yellow blooms a beautiful sight.

Nestled on the slopes of Monte Subasio, Assisi came into view from miles away. It probably had not changed since St. Francis (born 1181) walked those roads. Everything there was about this beloved saint: the basilica was actually two fine 13th-century churches, one on top of the other, with frescoes celebrating the life of St. Francis. Most important of these was a series of twenty-eight frescoes by Giotto, the first major Renaissance artist. Even more exquisite were the paintings by Simone Martini of Sienna.

There also was the Piazza del Commune as well as the remains of the Temple of Minerva.

There was one splendid hotel, Subasio, which had been converted from a 12th-century monastery. It was essential to try the local wine and food and witness the most incredible views from the dining room, where one could see forever! When we finally took our leave, it was to Padova and the famous Albano Therme. We drove through Perugia, Florence, and Bologna before we finally reached Padova, which was our final destination in Italy. We now headed for a well-deserved rest.

Albano is a typical spa town, where the wealthy used to come from all around Europe to "take the waters." The town has over one hundred thermal pools, and features much venerated "mud therapy." It is filled with luxurious hotels, restaurants and boutiques, cafés, parks, and music.

It seemed so much part of a bygone era. Elegantly dressed strollers roamed the streets any time of day or night, shopping, or simply passing the time, or listening to music at the bandstand.

We stayed a day in Padova, where Shakespeare set the *Taming of the Shrew*. It would have been much the same in his time. It had one of the earliest universities in Italy, founded in 1222, located right in the historic center near the Palazzo della Ragione, known as "Il Salone" because of its immense size. It is the largest medieval building existing in Europe, built around 1218 as the house of government. It was reconstructed in 1306 by Frau Giovanni degli Eremitani, who designed the roof as an upturned boat, which was covered by frescoes by Giotto and his workshop. The church by the same architect dates from 1276, and retains some fresco fragments from the 14th century. An important stop was Café Pedrocchi, which is very theatrical and houses art galleries. After spending the day "taking the waters," soaking in the various pools, getting massages, and being pampered, we were ready for the trip back to Vienna via Salzburg.

What a shock it was to go from mild Italy, in the eighties, all the way down to the thirties as we reached some of the higher elevations in the Alps. By early afternoon, when we stopped for lunch, there was snow on the ground!

We arrived back at Mother's apartment by early evening, ready to welcome the newly arrived spring in Vienna. What an incredible range of climates we experienced in a single day! We celebrated Mother's eighty-second birthday in Grinzing at her favorite tavern. There was live gypsy music, and we sang along as they played her favorite songs, and even shed some tears of joy. She was all aglow and savored every minute, ignoring the fatigue she surely felt.

Vienna, 1997

≈

We three sisters sat at Mother's bedside in the hospital room looking at each other. There were many unanswered questions and unsolved mysteries waiting for replies. Mother had suddenly collapsed a few days earlier. Even in this state, she looked so refined in her well-chosen jewelry; her complexion remarkably smooth for her eighty-five years; her Chanel fragrance permeating her whole being. From her finely chiseled face, only her eyes told the story. She was just skin and bones, having lost all the roundness that had given her such allure. She wore a soft cashmere jacket tied with a satin ribbon at the neckline, so sweet! There was elegance to her being in every setting. She was pain free, but her heart was tired; it was beating without it's natural rhythm, preparing to slow down for the end of her journey. Her mind was clear, but she could see the world closing in on her. Her memory was selective; some things are best forgotten—it's easier that way. We were in a sterile, bare hospital room, hoping for a little more time. There had been a constant thread connecting us in our individual lives. We shared memories, some poor, missing many details. Only Mother had the answers, but would there be time to find them out?

We sink into the past, the long ago, a time much forgotten and yet still remembered …

Mother was a monarchist. She felt that the German language, which was mandatory in all Habsburg nations, united us all. The union of the Austro-Hungarian Empire connected many of the lesser communities, providing jobs, education, and opportunities, however unequal. At the same time, the individual countries were allowed to use their own cultural preferences and retain autonomy. She spoke several languages, which was necessary considering the close proximity and intermingling of these nations. She saw this as the beginning of the EU, which happened much later.

Mother never accepted the communist doctrines, and was concerned for her eldest, Edith, because she had been educated in that philosophy, along with Edith's young son, Laci, who never knew any other way of thinking. She had learned to cope with the overwhelming trauma of being separated from her children by creating a total emotional barrier to her feelings. She had shut them out completely in order to survive. Sometimes, seeing young children in the park on the swings would send her into a crying fit, but she was tough and recovered.

Betty, the youngest of her daughters, had received the least motherly love in her life, which she still craves. Now, in the hospital room, she anticipated Mother's every wish, jumping up and smoothing her pillow, offering her a drink of water, or just holding her hand.

Life was cruel to Betty. She was born as we were on our way to escape from Hungary to go to Aunt Mila's. It was March 30, 1945, when the Russian soldiers were already marching into Hungary. Poor Mother, with the help of a midwife in a strange little hamlet, delivered a little curly-haired angel at ten that night. Father, in the meantime, had returned back home to bring food for us all, as were now stranded. He discovered that the bridges across the Danube had all been destroyed by the retreating German army. He gathered what food he found and was able to carry, and started back on this harrowing journey, climbing over the remaining structures, and crossing over the fast current of the river. On April 1, 1945, Easter Sunday, sirens began their shrieking sounds, and we all had to run for the shelter, leaving Mother and her newborn infant alone. It was war! We were somewhat prepared with food and water, candles, and blankets. It was ten in the morning when the Russian troops arrived, and they did as many victors do in a war: they stripped homes of all valuables, forcefully raped young women, and destroyed whatever came their way. One of the drunken soldiers found Mother and her baby, and was about to rape her, but she fought to protect her child, like a lioness in nature! Fortunately, an officer came to her rescue, grabbed the drunken man, and threw him out the window. Mother was grateful. He asked her if it was a boy or a girl, and she was able to communicate with him in Russian. The officer took out his wallet and showed her his children's picture with tears in his eyes. He ordered a guard to watch for her safety.

A Trip Out West, August of 1999

≈

It was August 31st, and the leaves started turning in Maine. Joe and I decided to visit the west and Joe's birthplace. We flew out of Portland, Maine, to Seattle, where we rented a car to drive to Vancouver, British Colombia. Vancouver is an intriguing city, blending British service with American plumbing, a most desirable combination. Once we arrived, we searched for the best spot to watch the sunset. It was from the Sheraton Hotel's revolving restaurant and lounge, where we were treated to a most memorable sunset and prolonged afterglow. As night fell, millions of lights reflected off the water like twinkling stars—what a sight to behold! I compare Vancouver to Rio de Janeiro, Hong Kong, or San Francisco, with mountain peaks dropping dramatically into the sea below, creating remarkable beauty.

We walked back to our hotel along Market Street, with its myriad boutiques, galleries, and cafés, where life goes on well past midnight. (So unlike Maine, where life shuts down at sunset.) We rejoiced in the nightlife in the cities, and checked out the nightclubs, music venues, and theaters. Joe was very active for his age and loved to see it all. The next day, we visited Canada Place, and stopped at some galleries and bookstores to stock up on reading material. Then we drove to the ferry and headed for Victoria, the capital of B.C., on Vancouver Island. It is so very British, with flower baskets hanging everywhere, picturesque buildings, a busy harbor, and the elegant Parliament Buildings. We explored all! Our hotel was across the harbor, with a state-of-the-art fitness center and spa, of which we took full advantage. We got massages and facials. We could choose between walking or taking the harbor ferry, which ran every fifteen minutes, to the center of town.

We took the ferry to Port Angeles, then found our way to Hurricane Ridge. It was a beautiful, sunny day, so we had to take a side trip into the Olympic mountain range, where we hiked the well-marked trails. We hurried to catch the five thirty ferry from Bainbridge Island to Seattle, and then drove on to Snoqualmie, where we had made reservations at the lovely Salish Lodge. We settled into our spacious room, took a jacuzzi, and drank flutes of champagne in the immense tub. I even lit some candles for a more romantic effect. Than we dressed for dinner and watched the sunset over Snoqualmie Falls. We were treated to an exquisite meal, with the chef coming to our table to inquire about our experience. The following day, after a scrumptious brunch, we drove into Mount Rainier National Park, where again we hiked the picturesque trails and took many pictures of the majestic peaks. Mount Rainier is approximately seven thousand feet at the peak.

Our next surprise came at the Gregson Fairmount Hot Springs, where we stayed for the night. The facility was equal to the best European spas. I will never forget sliding down the four-story waterslide into one of the four pools of varying temperatures, and swimming at night under splendid star-filled skies, with only crickets and birds to serenade us. It was surprising that none of the travel books even mentioned these hot springs. We found them by sheer accident.

We spent a day at Glacier National Park—where Joe's grandfather had been the engineer who had built the roads—especially the "Going-to-the-Sun Highway," with its steep, sharp curves. This beautiful park deserves a lot more than a day's visit. There was so much beauty to see!

I was especially delighted by the mountain goats leaping high above on the cliffs. We drove back to Seattle and flew to Kalispell, Montana, Joe's birthplace. You needed to have a camera ready when flying between two peaks through the narrow opening leading to the landing strip, just past the water's edge. There was so much beauty below: the huge lake, the mountains, the beginning of fall colors, and a lake so clear you could see pebbles in it from the air.

Kalispell is located in Flathead Valley; it is named after the large lake. Flathead Lake is completely surrounded by mountains. Glaciers gleam in the early morning sunrise, and there are the bluest skies as far as the eye can see. This is why it's called "Big Sky Country," for the immenseness of the place is staggering. We were there on a perfect day, in the low seventies, with cool, crisp nights. We drove on to Moiese and the National Bison Ranch, where we watched a video about the area. Then we drove on to the high roads, seeing many different animals before coming upon a large heard of bison right in front of us. A photo opportunity!

Anaconda, with its many mines, was also fascinating, and I learned that it was all owned by a Hungarian immigrant. There were signs of splendid homes, which indicated a prosperous past during the gold rush days, but now this was just a memory.

Next stop was the state capital, Helena, and we saw a great C.M. Russell painting. We also stopped at the art museum, which was filled with Russell's work. Then we moved on to Great Falls, Montana, C.M. Russell's hometown. The museum there had one of the largest collections of western art, including Remington and the work of actor/artist George Montgomery. We stopped at an Indian reservation in Vaughn, drove the scenic road back to Kalispell, and took a flight back to Seattle for yet another day of discovery in this colorful port city. We admired the markets and waterfront, savored some seafood, and finally returned to Portland, Maine, where fall was in full bloom. The leaves turned to orange and yellow and purple and red; the nights were cool enough to enjoy the fireplace.

Finding Our Home in Sarasota, 1994

≈

When we got married, Joe had a place in Palm Springs, which he and his first wife had rarely used. Only friends and business associates stayed there. We visited once, and I told Joe to sell it. They also owned a charming villa in Hilton Head at Sea Pines. We stayed there once or twice, but I saw Hilton Head as a place for boating, tennis, and golf, none of which interested me. After enjoying a pleasant vacation, I told Joe it was not the place I wanted to retire. He and Louise had been big tennis players, even sponsors of the Family Circle tennis tournaments. The villa was rented out when they did not use it, but I asked him to sell that also.

We spent a few weeks every year, sometimes even twice a year, at the active Regency Health Spa, located in Hallandale Beach, Florida. This was a place where Joe and I were able to relax, stop drinking coffee and alcohol, and detox. With plenty of healthy vegan food, and plenty of physical activity in the fresh ocean breezes, we always came away rejuvenated.

In 1999, I was diagnosed with sarcoma (a cancer). As soon as I had the lumpectomy, I rushed to the Regency Spa, where I undertook a twenty-eight-day water fast under the supervision of health director, Dr. Frank Sabatino. My body was completely healed and restored to wellness. Dr. Sabatino advocated fasting for many illnesses, explaining that when all of the body's energy turns to healing instead of digesting, homeostasis is restored.

My first visitor was my son, Rod. We took long walks on the beach in the sunshine, and connected in a very special way as adults. Joe also came to stay and found me fully recovered. The best part of the fast was that my taste buds were renewed! The first meal I had was a slice of watermelon, and I had never tasted flavors so fully and completely before.

Joe and I visited Sarasota. As a boy, his aunts had lived there on Rose Street, and he remembered how much he liked it. His aunts, who wintered in Sarasota and summered in Maine, had belonged to the Sarasota arts community. We agreed that we would retire here when he was ready. On one of our trips to the spa, Joe suggested I fly over to Sarasota and find a place to rent for the coming winter. I arranged for a realtor to meet me at the airport to show me what was available. After hunting for two days and finding nothing I liked, I was very disappointed. I called the only person I knew in Sarasota, who was an old Hungarian friend. She suggested I call Judy Kepetcz who would show me just what I wanted. I immediately called Judy, and we met first thing in the morning. She listened and understood what we wanted: a comfy place on the beach. She proceeded to drive me to the south end of Lido Key to look at an empty property that had only a trailer on it for a sales office. We looked at proposed layouts. It was to be called L'Elegance on Lido Key.

Next she drove me to L'Ambiance on Long Boat Key. This building was already finished, occupied, and developed by the same builder. Judy recommended we buy pre-construction to get a good price. I fell in love with what I saw, and knew the new condo they were developing would be just as perfect. I happily rushed back to show Joe what I had found. He was every bit as excited. We poured over the plans, and decided to get the largest unit on a high floor to have the best views. We purchased on the tenth floor. It took two years for L'Elegance to be completed, and we had to choose some of the finishes, tiles, cabinets, etc., which required we spend some time nearby.

At this point, we rented a three-bedroom place for the winter only two doors away from L'Elegance. Then I flew to Vienna to collect Mother and bring her back to join us in Sarasota. This was November 1994. The day we were to leave Vienna, however, Mother collapsed with a stroke. I called 911, and within minutes she received oxygen and was rushed to the hospital. I called her physician, who met us at the hospital. After acupuncture treatments and high vitamin infusions, she was ready to travel within a month.

This was the first Christmas Mother had spent in Florida, surrounded by her children, grandchildren and some great grandchildren. It was a very happy occasion.

Mother enjoyed the warm winter climate. She had always been a swimmer, and now she could swim every day in the lovely pool, get plenty of sunshine, and eat some great seafood, which she savored. We found her a good acupuncturist, Harvey Kaltsis, and a Hungarian hairdresser, with whom she could communicate. She even had her cataracts removed by an eye doctor who specialized in that.

It came time to take Mother back to Vienna, and again I accompanied her on this long journey—Sarasota, Tampa, Augusta, New York, Vienna! She returned to her friends and life in Vienna with many happy memories of her trip.

The following winter, in 1995, our condo was still not finished, so Joe proposed to take Mother and me to Egypt for the winter. We were already in Vienna for Christmas, and we all wanted to see the pyramids and the history connected with Egypt. The mild climate helped to convince us along with all the history we could get immersed in.

Again we traveled first class. In Cairo, we stayed in the center so we could visit the fantastic museum. Then we moved out to the famous Mena House, by the pyramids, where so many celebrities and writers as well as archaeologists have stayed. It was a well-preserved, simply elegant hotel, and we spent several nights there while touring the pyramids with our guide. We visited all the important sites, and did a Nile cruise, where most of the passengers fell sick with dysentery. Joe had the dining room to himself, for he never got sick. Again we found places with swimming pools that served interesting food. We traveled in feluccas (local sailboats), where we heard fascinating stories from our guide. It was a most rewarding winter that brought much shorter flights for Mother, and many new memories to treasure.

Fortunately, Mother spent the winter of 1996 here in our new condo with both Edith and Betty visiting, along with her grandchildren and great grandchildren. That fall, our home was completed and furnished and lived in. I was so glad she was able to enjoy it! She really liked Sarasota, our friends and neighbors, the opera. She especially enjoyed the pool, swimming almost daily.

Saunders Manufacturing

～

Joe's company, which had started as a family business back in 1944, had grown, and by now had representatives from Maine to California. Joe very fortunately hired a great sales person, John Rosmarin, who eventually became president of the company.

Around this time, in the late nineties, a lot of American manufacturing was moved to China, where labor was cheap. Our company board voted to move some of our manufacturing from Maine to China, in spite of Joe's apprehension. The vice president and production manager traveled to China and made the arrangements. Joe and I soon visited Hong Kong and Mainland China, where the manufacturing was being done. Unfortunately, the Chinese had quickly copied our products and became competitors with a cheapened version of the original. Joe decided to return the production to the USA. He purchased a property in Meridian, Mississippi because it was near the port for shipping and also centrally located for delivery.

We flew to Meridian when the purchase was complete and all contracts signed, and we began the renovation of the huge warehouse, which had been a factory for mobile homes. The floors were covered with tar, and we physically worked at scraping and removing it. This purchase was a brilliant move! It came in handy because, during times of low sales, the rental of some of the space helped the company's bottom-line. Joe and I spent six months living at the Holiday Inn, the nicest hotel in town at the time, where we ate southern cuisine and met some lovely people. The fitness facility was first class and located in the hospital, so I spent a lot of my free time there. We finally decided to buy a home, which Joe thought might be used by visiting employees from Maine. However, this never happened. Once again, I had another home to furnish and decorate. It was not an easy task because the nearest furniture store was in Jackson. I also took many shopping trips to Birmingham, Alabama, since Meridian did not have much in the way of stores.

Joe rehired a former employee, Theron White, to run the Mississippi company, and also hired a handicapped workshop to do some easy assembly. This gave the company a nice tax break. Now we had another house, one of my favorites, with a central entry, a great room with a huge fireplace and mantel. It had two bedrooms and two bathrooms, a living room, a dining room, and a nice kitchen. The best part was the garden with two huge magnolia trees, which gave plenty of shade in the steamy summers.

To decorate the house, I used all of Joe's western art collection, which was in pastel colors.

We befriended our neighbors, had some fun parties, and even spent a Thanksgiving there with daughter Charmaine, and Theron and his wife. But once we realized we were not using the house anymore, we sold it. That is why, when we purchased our condominium in Sarasota, we had it furnished from our stuff in storage. Luckily, everything fit perfectly, and I still live with some of those pieces. All of the oriental rugs on the floor came from the house in Meridian. I called it the Pink House because I used a lot of soft pinks on the walls.

A Family Reunion, 2003

≈

The family decided it was time to get together at our heavenly spot in Maine, a place where we could accommodate everyone. Joe had added a studio to the three-car garage, where he was going to paint. He very wisely installed heating and added a complete bathroom so that it could serve as an additional guest room, even though we already had a guesthouse. Daughter Peggy had built it on the property for herself, and shared it with a friend until she realized she wanted to live alone. It was a lovely two-story A-frame with a wrap-around wooden deck.

It had three bedrooms and two baths, with a full basement for storage, and a large dining room and kitchen. Joe's secretary, Betty, and her husband rented it for years until our grandson, West, got married. Then he and his new bride, Kathy, moved in and lived there for several years. It was so nice to watch their daughter, Ryle, grow. Eventually, West started working for Saunders Manufacturing in the art department, and it was very convenient for him to live so close to work. At the time of the reunion, West and Kathy had moved away to be closer to her family. They were expecting a second child, and the guesthouse became empty and available for our family and guests.

My nephew, Laci, the Olympic athlete, even invited a close family friend from Hungary, who stayed in a nearby B and B. There were family members from Chicago, Texas, Budapest, and Arizona, and for the first time, we could all be together in one location. Edith came with her close friend, Tony; Betty arrived with Joe Vaghetto; and Kathryn brought her husband, Greg, and daughter, Alexis. Both Tony and Joe were excellent cooks and prepared a lot of the meals. We waterskied, and I even taught some to windsurf, kayak, canoe, and use the paddleboat. Everyone swam, played games, drank, and ate good food. We explored the whole area, even taking trips to Acedia National Park, which had a 360-degree view from the top.

We had a lot of fun. Rod occupied the art studio with Max and Joy; Charmaine and her family stayed in the main house with us; Betty's group all stayed in the guest house with Laci and his girlfriend.

I believe everyone was happy that they'd come, and left with a smile and a nice suntan. Summers in Maine are unbeatable! That's why so many friends and family visited often. It was the best place to enjoy summer, with warm days and cool nights and fresh lobster. We had an extensive library, so visitors could hang out and read and enjoy the peace and quiet. At nights, we lay on the deck and counted falling stars, or just told stories of times passed.

Returning to Our Roots, 2009

≈

(The family: Charmaine, Adam, Natalie, Jamie, Max, Joy, Joe, and I; sorely missing was Rod!) For Christmas, 2008, we gave the Goldman family a trip to Austria and Hungary so I could show them their roots. I enlisted sister Edith, who had made a B and B right in the center of Vienna. It was the apartment where Mother used to live, which was our second home. She agreed to keep the dates open for us, as well as the B and B she had in Budapest, which at the time, was managed by her son, Laci. It was Laci who agreed to plan out our activities, with plenty of swimming and educational highlights, visits to friends' homes, and such fun diversions as the Renaissance fair at the castle of Sumeg, which we all attended wearing costumes of the period.

Joe and I arrived in Vienna on July 30th, and Edith had wonderful food waiting for us at the B and B at Borseplatz. The next day, Edith and I shopped and baked sweet rolls with poppy seeds and walnuts in preparation for the kids' arrival.

When the last pan was removed from the oven, Edith and I went swimming in the Danube. The river was cold, and it had a swift current. I had to swim hard, but it was so refreshing. Nothing like swimming in the raw—it feels so right. We remembered the days when we did plenty of skinny-dipping in the Lajta, the river behind our property in Magyarovar, our hometown. We dried off and took a train and a streetcar back to Borseplatz. It was late, and I slept until I heard noises from the dining room. Edith was serving her guests a Viennese breakfast, which is quite an elaborate feast! After our meal we took a streetcar to the Nashmarkt, where we loaded up on fresh fruits and vegetables and cheeses. We even found some Herend plates in the Queen Victoria pattern, which my daughter collected, so I had to buy them. We were now prepared to go and meet the kids at the airport.

There was so much joy in seeing each other in a strange land. For the grandkids, this was their first trip overseas. We had to take a cab, for we could not all fit in the large van Laci had rented. We all arrived at Edith's B and B, and after the initial tour, we picked out our rooms and then sat down to a scrumptious meal of Hungarian specialties. We ate until bursting. After dinner, I took Max and Jamie down to the playground across the street, which even had a zip line, while the rest of the group went swimming in the Danube.

The next day, we took a city tour with our local friend and teacher, Marlene. It was hot, so we cooled off in St. Stephansdom, the beautiful cathedral in the center of the city, where we climbed the bell tower for a better view. We spent a full day of sightseeing in the hot city.

The third day, we all took a trip to Mosonmagyarovar, Hungary, my hometown, where we were welcomed by the Polonyi family. They are very special friends, since Nandi and Betty share a birthday. Nandi was the perfect host, and his lovely wife, Agnes, had prepared a feast for us. Their kids, Milan, thirteen, and July, twenty-two, joined us in a little tour of my hometown.

There is no greater joy than being able to share a little piece of the past and the memories of one's childhood with those we love!

We then started out for Halaszi, and a boat ride on the river. Unfortunately, it had been a rainy summer and the mosquitos were biting. After the boat trip, we went to shoot bows and arrows, with both Max and Joy showing a real aptitude for shooting. Edith, Charmaine, and I watched the fun and took pictures until the sunset, when we headed back to Vienna. Since we had all worked up an appetite, we stopped near the Austrian border at Paprikas Csarda, a tavern with excellent food. We ate all of our favorites: vadas with dumplings, a sweet-and-sour preparation of venison, chicken paprika with spaetzle, and other Hungarian delights. We all enjoyed the feast and arrived back in Vienna, tired and ready to drop into bed.

On day four, the weather was rainy. As Laci and the four kids and I started out for the Natural History Museum, we got caught in a downpour and then found the museum closed. So we went to the Hundertwasser House by car instead, where we watched a movie about this forward-thinking artist and had lunch in the café. Next visit was the Hofburg to visit Sissy's apartments in the Royal Palace, the home of the Habsburg rulers. Sissy was the wife of Franz Joseph, the last of the Habsburg emperors. She was very popular with the people, for she was young and beautiful and loved nature, which was where she often escaped from the demands of her role as empress. This turned out to be a good history lesson for the kids in a very interesting, elaborate setting. We got home in time for dinner. Max and Jamie went to bed, and the rest of us walked to the Rathausplatz to watch opera on the big screen.

In summers in Vienna, a big screen is set up at city hall park each night. The program varies from rock and pop to classical and opera. Food is served in the surrounding area, and people come to make a night of it. The time we were there, it rained off and on all evening, but we enjoyed it anyway.

Day five, we made a stop at the outlet mall near the border, and everyone found something wonderful to purchase. Then we were on our way to the thermal baths in our hometown, again with the Polonyi family. There were many different pools of varying temperatures, and some had water massage. There was also a wave pool, my favorite! We were the last to leave at closing. We returned to the Lucsony Restaurant—Nandi had made reservations there in advance. By the time we finished, said goodbyes, and drove back to Vienna, it was very late.

The next day, we all slept in, and we had no special plans. It was a free day in Vienna! We all went in different directions. I spent the morning with Joe, who was going to remain in Vienna with Edith while we were going on to Hungary and the rest of the tour. As I walked along the street, I ran into Cookie and the girls, who were lost. I took them to visit Meinl, the most beautiful delicatessen in the world! We gathered back for lunch, and I took a trip to the new fitness center to try out the Power Plate, which I found amazing. On my return, we all loaded into the van, and off we went to the Krapfenwaldbad, which we never found. We ended up on top of Kalenberg, just in time for sunset and a beautiful view of the city from up high on the mountaintop. From here, we drove to Grinzing, the Viennese wine growing area. We chose one of the many old taverns from the 15th century, where we found a big table for the ten of us. There was live music, excellent local wine, and good food.

Day six, we left Austria for ten days in Hungary. Each of us was only allowed one small backpack for all our needs, due to the lack of space in the van. This time Joe and Edith stayed in Vienna, and only the eight of us left.

By the time we arrived in Csorna, the planned horseback riding was out of the question. The owner claimed it was too hot for the horses, at 92 degrees Fahrenheit. Laci and the kids were disappointed but soon forgot all about it when we went swimming in Lipot waterpark. There were hot thermal pools and a warm children's pool with waves and waterslides.

The drive to Tapolca was long, and we had to stop to refuel our bellies. We arrived at our lodgings, a lovely old hotel, where we had four rooms on the second floor. We happily settled in for the next three days.

On day seven, after a sumptuous breakfast, we toured the town and visited Herend, one of the most famous places in Hungary. Here, beautiful porcelain is made, which was collected by royalty in the last century and now is world famous. We enjoyed the tour and watched how the pieces were hand-painted and designed.

Next we got into our costumes for the festival, which Laci had provided from his large collection. It was a stifling summer day when we started up the mountain in our extremely hot velvet and leather clothes. However, it was worth the sweat and tears when people took our pictures and thought we were part of the entertainment, so we got in for free! Up in the old castle, which is now in ruins, we saw an amazing performance by Italian flag throwers; it was like being in the Middle Ages. Then we rushed down the mountain to watch jousting, fencing on horseback, and juggling. It was all so much fun, but the highlight for my family was the kurtos kalacs, which is a specialty food for outdoor events. It is a flaky dough that is wrapped around a metal rod about three inches in diameter and twenty inches long, with a handle for turning. It is turned over an open fire, then rolled into sugar and turned some more, and as it is turned over the flames, the sugar caramelizes over the pastry and is crunchy, sweet, and yummy. When the show ended, we drove back to Tapolca for dinner. Another full day of fun!

On day eight, I got up for an early walk, and met with Cookie and Adam, who had the same idea, so we toured this charming small town together. Next we visited the caverns, which had been carved out by water over thousands of years. We climbed down the hundreds of steps to the boats. Only two persons per boat were allowed since the water was very shallow. We all enjoyed cooling off on this hot day; the temperatures were a great deal less than outside.

Our next stop took us to Sumeg, where the girls went horseback riding with Laci, the expert. He had represented the USA in the modern pentathlon in two consecutive Olympic games: swimming, fencing, running, shooting, and equestrian. He had to be good in all five sports, which takes real dedication.

The rest of us toured the Bishop's mansion and museum, and went for a wine tasting at the Bishop's wine cellar, deep down in the earth. As we descended, so did the temperature. We sat around the "round table" and tasted some nice local wines.

Now we were ready for a swim. As we checked the map, we realized we were not far from the famous Heviz, which boasts as the largest thermal lake in Europe. This was a new experience for most of the group. We rented inner tubes and floated around enjoying the healthy waters. We had to rush back to Tapolca, where we had made reservations for dinner on the lake, and watched a concert being performed on the stage right over the water.

The show was wonderful, even better from our front row seats. Rain began just as the show ended, so we had to move indoors to finish our meal, which again was a culinary delight!

Day nine was a Monday, and the girls wanted to check out the local shops, which they could only admire through the windows over the weekend. We picked up some pogacsa, a tasty cheese biscuit for a snack on the road.

Next destination was Tihany, the highest point overlooking Lake Balaton, which is the largest inland lake in Europe. Then we took the ferry across the lake to meet the Korodi family, local friends of Laci's.

We met at a unique country inn, Csarda, which specialized in a spicy, Hungarian fish stew. After our troop was all filled, we drove on to the beach for a swim and boating on Lake Velence, where we met Ocsi, the eighteen-year-old son of Laci's friend, Steven. We all happily jumped in for a quick swim in the refreshing water to cool off before we changed clothes for a city tour of Szekesfehervar, the original capital of Hungary. First, our host Steven recommended that we sample the best ice cream in town, then he treated us to a history lesson before we followed him to his home in an appealing neighborhood on the outskirts of the city. Tunde, Steven's wife, was awaiting us with a big spread of sweets and fruit. It was wonderful to see their lovely garden. We even picked some ripe pears from the trees, which were in season—a special activity for city kids. Before long, it was time to say goodbye and head for Budapest, our home for the next few days.

We were a tired group even with naps along the way. Once in this grand city, Laci gave us a little night drive around, and you could not help but gasp at the magnificent sight of Budapest at night. The graceful Chain Bridge sparkled its reflection in the Danube. The Parliament glowed in its full nighttime glory, and the Freedom Statue was brightly lit up on top of Mount Gellert. Many brightly shining boats floated on the river, which reflected back all the lights. For someone arriving for the first time, the beauty of the capital of this much-tormented country is unexpected. It was well after midnight when we finally retired in our new lodging, one of Edith's B and Bs in this city, which comfortable slept all of us.

On day ten of our trip, Laci and I drove to a large supermarket to load up on groceries. After a big brunch, we got on the streetcar for our city viewing and then we went on to the castle just as it started to rain. We walked around the Fisherman's Bastion and saw the beauty of this ancient city in the rain. We hurried home since we had plans for the evening. While I prepared dinner, Laci collected his daughter, Vivien, who joined us for the performance at eight. It was a colorful folk-dance group with authentic costumes of the region from which the dances originated. Music was by a gypsy band, which was very entertaining. It was all clear when we left the theater, and some of us returned back to our rooms, while the rest went on to a nighttime cruise on the Danube.

After a good night's rest, some of us chose to take the streetcar to an amusement park that was much the same as it had been in my childhood days. We all enjoyed the rides, even Charmaine and I going on some, and when we'd had enough, we started for the streetcar. On the way, in the middle of the park, was a charming lake with swans and ducks swimming in it and a lovely restaurant right over the water. We stopped for a rest and a bite as we watched the baby ducks swimming.

The older members opted for a rock concert on the island in the Danube, which is huge and attracts the youth from all over Europe. Adam and Natalie left early:

the noise, the thick mass of humanity, and the heavy drug and alcohol consumption frightened the thirteen year old Natalie. She had never been to anything like it before.

On day eleven, we were still going strong, and I left early to get some freshly baked strudels for breakfast at the nearby bakery. After breakfast, we made a twelve o'clock appointment to tour the Parliament. To my surprise, I was still considered a citizen and got in free. The tour was very special and educational in this very opulent place, with the highlight being the royal crown and its many precious stones sparkling. We also visited the museum of ethnology, but the girls spotted a dress shop and disappeared into it. Next we visited the beautiful art deco New York Café. It had been purchased by an Italian and painstakingly restored to its original glory.

Then we drove to pick up cousin Vivie, and met her mother, Andrea, Laci's ex. Andrea was an Olympian in rhythmic gymnastics and was still coaching the Hungarian team in the sport.

Our next adventure took us to StEndre, a large artist colony just thirty minutes from the city, with many galleries, studios, boutiques, and cafés, lively and colorful and always packed with visitors. It stretches along the Danube and has a unique atmosphere. We walked all over, visited the peaceful little church, and found a lovely restaurant by the river, where we enjoyed the cool breezes. There was live music, and some of us got up and danced. It was such a wonderful way to introduce my family to this special little part of the world I called home.

On day twelve, we separated; Charmaine, Adam, and the teens visited the House of Terror museum, the very prison where both Charmaine's father, Emery, and her grandmother, Mausi, were tortured and imprisoned. They sobbed through the whole tour as they watched videos from survivors. It is painful to see the cruelty of one human being toward another. We received a call from them as they started their subway trip back home: they had been stopped and held because their ticket had expired by two hours. Laci came to their rescue, and was very upset with the guard who detained them instead of helping them when they had asked for his help. Not a good way to handle tourists.

It was day thirteen when we started out early to visit Sass Hegy, where I'd gone to boarding school at age six—Notre Dame de Sion, a Catholic, French boarding school, which was shut down during the communist era when all religious education had stopped. The nuns had been sent back to France, and Mother Superior had been detained and imprisoned.

Next we climbed up to the Citadel, the statue representing freedom, on top of Mount Gellert, to get some great views of the city below. Laci took us to his new residence he'd purchased for himself, with his Japanese toilet that had a seat warmer and other special features, and we all approved.

Our visit would not have been complete without visiting Vivien's dance studio and seeing her in action with her partner. She was an accomplished ballroom dancer. The two of them moved with such grace and ease while doing some intricate footwork; it was a joy to watch.

We then drove to a strand, which Vivien frequented, and changed into swimsuits for a refreshing swim in the Danube. After the sunset, when the mosquitos began to swarm, we requested a private room for the nine of us where we were safe from the bugs.

On day fourteen, the three teenage girls wanted to go shopping in a mall while the rest of us resumed sightseeing. We rode to Hero's Square, Vajdahunyad Castle, and returned to meet up with the girls in the mall. After a quick lunch there, we drove over to the oldest Roman Baths in the city; they had various indoor and outdoor pools, slides, saunas, and steam rooms (Turkish baths), and everybody enjoyed this experience. We had to rush to get to Margitsziget for a performance of Experidance Group. We just made it on time to the show, which was interesting. After saying goodbye to Vivien and dropping her back home, we returned to spend our last night in the Marvany utca B and B. It was time to go!

We called Joe and Edith in Vienna to see if they needed anything and to alert them of our return. On the way, we made a stop at Lake Balaton for a cooling swim, and again found kurtos kalacs, the newly acquired favorite food of the girls. Laci took us on the scenic route up to Pannonhalma, a monastery way up on a hill. It had gorgeous views and was surrounded by vineyards.

On the way to Vienna, we had to make one more stop at the Paprikas Tavern for a last Hungarian dinner, which was marvelous. It was very late when we arrived in Vienna, hauled all our stuff up by elevator, and crashed. Both Joe and Edith were happy to see us back, and we had many stories to tell!

It was day sixteen, and we were again in Vienna. We all slept late, and had a great Viennese brunch by Edith. I read my diary of the last eleven days' activities to Joe. Then we proceeded to take out old albums of family and relatives that the children had never met; their ancestors' pictures were shown and postcards were read, and they got a glimpse into their past.

It was time to find the Krapfenwaldbad up in the mountains—and success! It was much cooler up here in the higher altitude than it was in the city below: a chance to enjoy the cool waters from the mountain springs. After we changed, it was dinnertime, and we picked one of the oldest inns in the city, the Griechenbeisl, dating from 1490. After another culinary delight, we walked over to the best Italian ice shop in the city before going home.

Day seventeen was the kids' last day in Vienna, so we all started packing. There was time for a walk to the Hotel Sacher for a takeaway torte, and one last stop in the world-famous café for a last Viennese memory. We even ran into friends, which shows how small the world has become. Time to crash for the early morning flight and goodbyes to all.

Once the family had left, it was very quiet. Edith's friend and boarder, Wolfgang Benheim (who is a prince), presented us with wine from his vineyard. Then he enthralled us with pictures of his family, the castle where he grew up, and the castle of his mother's family, which had been renovated. It had taken him ten years! He later began renovating the old family castle, which was even older and in more need of repair. It was a fascinating evening, and we enjoyed getting to know this interesting man.

We also visited our young friend Alex, then returned home to look at the two hundred pictures we took of our trip, before Laci drove back to Budapest and his life there. We stopped to see our friend Marlene, and Alex drove us to the airport for our flight home.

The first stop was Paris, and our flight got delayed, so we missed our connection at O'Hare Airport. When we finally arrived in Atlanta, we had to wait until the next day for our flight, so we had to stay at a Hilton for the night. Finally we made it back to our lovely home in Readfield, Maine. However, it was hard to get back to the routine of daily life after such a delicious break.

My Children, Charmaine Lisa and Rodney Steven

~

I am the very fortunate mother of two amazing children: Charmaine, the older, and Rod, the younger. They are so very different in personality and talents, like night and day!

Charmaine is a sweet, feminine, kind, caring daughter with a heart of gold, always thinking of everyone else. She is an exceptional mother to her two girls and a very good wife, cook, and housekeeper. She followed in my footsteps, giving up the corporate world to become a Pilates teacher. She chose the perfect husband in Adam, who is an asset to the family and also an amazing father. I am fortunate to have them in my life.

Son Rod is a very talented, creative person, who is good at so many things. He studied art and got his master's degree in bronze sculpting, a very difficult medium. However, when he could not make an adequate living teaching, he gave up his passion and turned to computer programming. He is also a self-taught musician and even had his own rock band for a while. Rod is a natural athlete—he played hockey well, was a great mountain-biker, and tried his hands at many different things. He has a great sense of humor and used to entertain us at family get-togethers with his jokes. I hope that he gets back to sculpting, for he is so very talented. I wish I could be closer to my son, for I love him very much and miss him.

My Grandchildren

~

The biggest joy in my life after having my own children are the wonderful grandchildren! Each has a unique personality and is so very special in a myriad of ways. I love each and every one of them. Our relationships began at their birth and grew through the many special occasions we celebrated together, the trips we enjoyed, and the memories we created. I made a promise to all of them that when they graduated from high school, each would get the trip of their choice.

The year was 2010 when Max was the first to graduate. He had a special love and interest in animals, so Joe suggested a trip to the Galapagos, with its numerous unique creatures. We had a splendid trip, delighting in the "blue-footed boobies," the smallest penguins, and giant lizards. The most memorable moment came, however, when Max was snorkeling. As he surfaced with his mask on, he found himself face-to-face with a sea lion. I have this recorded on camera!

The next graduate was Joy, in 2011, and she chose India! I had been there before I married Joe, in 1985, and was happy to return twenty-six years later to see the changes in this fast-developing country. My 1985 trip had been an amazing event. I was invited to travel with doctors and healers from the USA, there to exchange Eastern and Western healing practices. That trip had been led by Dr. Larry Dossey (the author of several books on healing) and his wife, Barbara.

In 2011 it was just Joy and me. It started with a big send-off by the Goldman's at O'Hare airport; even Nancy and Emery Homor came!

We had a five-star trip from beginning to end, with our own driver and a black Mercedes. My first surprise was the brand new airport in Delhi. Upon our arrival, the temperature was 45 degrees Celsius. We had a chance to stay in a maharaja's hunting lodge, where we took a jeep safari and saw the elusive white tiger, a jaguar, and many other creatures big and small. We visited the Taj Mahal at sunrise, and saw the pink city of Jaipur, a city famous for its silk. We shopped for just the right silver necklace that Joy wanted as a souvenir, and looked for some beautiful silks and other fabrics to bring home. We even had a chance to ride the train, an unforgettable experience in India. We rode in a rickshaw and on an elephant, and visited a home for street kids, who had been abandoned.

We always stayed in elegant hotels with swimming pools and excellent Indian food, which we both enjoyed. When we had dysentery, our driver told us to have only water and bananas, which he provided. In Udaipur, we had the most unusual accommodations—peacocks and deer walked the grounds, and there were some wild animals in cages and enclosures.

In Rajasthan, we visited the Royal Gardens, and took a boat ride to the Monsoon Palace in the middle of the lake. These were just some of the highlights of this enchanted land. The long flight was made comfortable by traveling business class. I know Joy learned a lot and hopefully will apply it in her life.

Natalie's turn came in 2014 when she graduated from high school. She was most interested in history, so we began our trip in Rome, followed by a land tour of Turkey and Greece, after which we boarded a little Greek cruise ship operated by Homeric Tours. We island-hopped around some of the more remote Greek Islands, since we could get into ports that the bigger cruise ships could not. Most remarkable was the popular Santorini, where we enjoyed a catamaran ride to different beaches to swim and climbed up a volcano with flip-flops. Ouch! We ate some fantastic Turkish and Greek meals. It was an educational trip for both of us. We were immersed in history, and it helped Natalie decide on her career choice.

Jamie, the youngest grandchild, graduated from high school in 2020, during the pandemic, so there was no real graduation or prom. She had to wait almost two years for her trip, when travel restrictions were somewhat lifted. She wanted to go to the British Virgin Islands, and selected Antigua. It was Princess Diana's favorite place to go with her boys. We stayed at the Royalton Antigua, an all-inclusive resort. We even had our own butler! Jamie chose to go on daylong boat trips around the island, stopping for picnics and snorkeling. We both enjoyed the pools and had our own section with Jacuzzis and water-aerobics classes. The highlight was snorkeling with stingrays and having our picture taken holding a big one!

Jamie enjoyed being able to order mimosas in the restaurant, watch great shows in the evenings, and even gamble in the casino, which she found exciting.

Because it was during the pandemic, we had to get tested both coming and going, which complicated travel.

These high school graduation trips provided a wonderful opportunity to spend valuable one-on-one time with each of my grandchildren! I treasure the experiences.

Selling Saunders Manufacturing

The year was 2008. Joe was in his eighties. It was time to sell the company and retire. He wanted to keep it right there in Maine, where it had all began. So many families had spent their whole lives working at Saunders Manufacturing. The best offer came from John Rosmarin, the company's president. Joe was happy, for he knew John would never move the company elsewhere. We decided it was time to sell the house as well, after spending our last summer there. It all worked out, and we sold just before the real estate market crashed. Now we had only our pleasant Sarasota home. By now, Joe had become accustomed to living in a condominium with many other people around, which was a big change from Maine. He spent at least an hour every morning walking in the pool with some of his buddies—Ed Schaffer, Norbert Heckert, Bob Fox, Alec Cass, Dennis, and John, just to name a few—while they solved the world's problems. He subscribed to all his favorite papers and passed them over the balcony to our next-door neighbors, the Kampens. Joe was an avid reader and singlehandedly supported the local bookstore Circle Books. After he died, so did the bookstore. He left me so many great books to read that it will take me another lifetime to finish them all.

While Joe enjoyed having breakfast at the Blue Dolphin, and made many friends in the community, I was busy teaching yoga at the Garden of the Heart studio or the Women's Resource Center or the Senior Friendship Center. I also taught water aerobics at the request of my friend Carol Peschel. I had taken the required certification classes and began teaching in our pool and the TBC pool on Longboat Key.

We had a close group of friends, the "originals" in the building, and enjoyed entertaining. We even started a gourmet club, and met regularly for dinners at each other's units. We also had some progressive dinners, just to compare each owner's decor. We called L'Elegance "the best kept secret on Lido." We received many visitors in the winter months, and still traveled but not so much, since we had such a full life here: operas, ballets, orchestras, theaters, even a circus, and an active social circle.

Joe and I took a couple of Caribbean cruises, but mainly took pleasure in our home and each other's company. We got involved with a concert series started by neighbors Jerry and Lee Doherty Ross right in their unit. It grew rapidly and moved to the lobby, and eventually to Holly Hall and on to the Ringling Museum's theater. Today the concerts are performed in several halls throughout the city as well as Venice, raising scholarship money for young talents. It was good to be part of such a worthwhile organization and watch it grow. This was all due to the energy and efforts of Lee and Jerry. I applaud them!

The End Is Near, 2014

Joe began to have some health concerns—sleep apnea at first, then breathing problems. As he gained weight, it became more serious. One night, he fell and hit his head on the marble floor. I called 911, and he was treated and transported to the hospital. This started his decline. He now needed an oxygen tank, a portable one so that he could move, but it was bulky and awkward, and he was not able to be active. Once he stopped his daily walks, his health worsened. He was still the happy, loving Joe, but he now had to preserve his energy. Fortunately, he spent a lot of time with his daughter Peggy, who previously had not been close to him but now enjoyed her father's company and his wisdom.

The diagnosis was COPD (chronic obstructive pulmonary disease). Once the oxygen from the portable tank was no longer sufficient, Joe was hospitalized. He was put on a high-flow oxygen machine, and I was told he would not last long since this was only a temporary fix. I was devastated, and spent days and nights with him, sleeping in an uncomfortable chair in his room. The doctors allowed me to bring him whatever he asked for to make him as comfortable as possible. He asked for a little cognac every night, and he got it! At one point, both son Harry and daughter Peggy were in the room with us to say their goodbyes. I never saw Harry again because he moved to North Carolina.

These were very difficult days for me. The hospital notified hospice, and Joe was given morphine to make him more comfortable as the high-flow machine no longer supplied the oxygen his lungs required; there was nothing more medicine could do for him. I climbed into bed with him and told him, "I love you very much, and you can let go. I would be OK." This was the hardest thing I ever did, but I knew I needed to release him so he could pass peacefully in my arms. My life was never the same; it took a turn, and I now live in a new phase—the "after Joe" phase.

A Tribute to Joe Saunders

Joseph Arthur Saunders: born July 9, 1926; died September 27, 2014

Joe was my incredibly wonderful husband, lover, and best friend. He taught me unconditional love. He was a cuddly teddy bear that you just had to adore. He was handsome, with the bluest blue, ever-smiling eyes, smooth fair skin, and a thick head of white hair, always neatly styled and combed. He was of medium height and extremely strong, with a great sense of humor—the New England kind. He lived his faith and did not need to go to church to worship. He demonstrated loving kindness to everyone he came in contact with. He could never pass a beggar without dropping some coins or bills to them. He made friends easily and was close to his business associates, with whom he made lifelong friendships.

He was interested in every subject, and was always open to listening to another's point of view. He listened intently when you spoke, and never interrupted even the most long-winded talker. He had the gift of making you very comfortable in his presence. He enjoyed playing the stock market, his way of gambling, he'd told me. He followed the stocks he selected and took pleasure in every win.

He was the most well-read person. After reading his three papers in the mornings—the *Wall Street Journal*, the *New York Times*, and the local *Observer*—he spent most of his free time reading. He spent hours in the little bookstore on St. Armands Circle and discussed new publications with the owners. They even asked him to review some of their new books, which he delighted in.

He was the most generous person. He loved to give little gifts for no reason, "just because," and always had my favorite flowers for any occasion, the fragrant lilies. He enjoyed life, loved his family, and delighted in making me happy! He liked the theater, loved music, and was very well-informed about composers. He also liked ballet and attended the opera with me every season. He told me, at the end of his life, that he never cared for the high-pitched soprano voices, but he came because I loved it. He had a beautiful singing voice and even took voice lessons, but only sang in the shower when no one could hear him. He was generous with his time. If one of the children needed advice, he always listened and helped them figure it out for themselves, which is what works.

He delighted in the finer things in life: fine food, excellent wines, the best of the best in alcohol or pastry. He knew how to make me happy!

One day, when he came home from the office and I was not there, he saw that my windsurfer was gone. He jumped in the boat and came to my rescue. I had become stranded as the wind died down and could not make my way back home. He dragged me and the windsurfer home by boat.

He started wearing bow ties on my encouragement, which became his trademark and earned him the nickname "Senator." He was my gift from God, the partner I prayed for after my divorce from my first difficult husband.

He loved unconditionally and restored my confidence in myself. He was so complimentary, acknowledging me for every little thing I did and supporting my studies to better myself. I am still working my way through the hundreds of books he left behind on every subject imaginable. There was no topic that he could not talk about: politics, finance, business, or world affairs. He was able to contribute to every subject and had an open mind to all points of view. He tried to paint, and even experimented with Japanese calligraphy.

Every time I drink a glass of wine, I think of his favorite saying: "Life is too short to drink bad wine." His tastes ran from French to South African. He took pleasure in life: good food, wine, conversation, and friends. He was always good at telling jokes.

I still miss his quiet, loving presence. I loved him deeply, and am so grateful for having had twenty-eight special years with him!

I had a memorial for celebrating this wonderful man's life, which I barely remember, I was so grief-stricken at the time. Fortunately, I had some good friends who helped me with all that needed to be done. The service was officiated by Unity Minister Elisabeth Thompson, who knew us well. The memorial was attended by family, friends, and neighbors. John Rosmarin, Walter Belden, and Theron White from Saunders Manufacturing came. Also there were our attorneys, Sumner Lipman and Norman Kominski, and many friends from the community. Sorely missing was son Harry Saunders. My son Rod represented the Homor family, and was a great support for me at this difficult time.

A Tribute to Emery Homor

≈

Emery Joseph Homor: born May 12,1927; died November 30, 2017

My first husband was a good man, a good father, and a good provider. He was ambitious and wanted the finer things in life, and was willing to do whatever it took to get them.

We met just a year after we both arrived in this country of freedom and opportunity. Emery had spent eight years of the most productive time of his life in communist prison, where all dignities were stripped away. Fortunately, he was freed by the revolution and escaped. We met after he and a friend, Nandi, had spent a difficult year washing walls at the Henry Ford Hospital in Detroit, Michigan. They were then offered scholarships to Roosevelt University in Chicago. My friend Mary, who helped newly arrived Hungarians find housing, was the one who introduced us. The two men intended to study accounting, which did not require exceptional language skills—their English was very poor.

When Emery asked me to marry him, it was out of survival that I accepted. I was not in love with him, but I knew I would be able to get out of the prison of my own life. We had a short engagement and a very small wedding with only the family present. I walked down the aisle with my veil covering my wet hair and quiet sobs coming from my heart. I guess he loved me in his own way, but was unable to express any emotion. Because of the big age difference, he elevated me to a pedestal and worshipped me from afar. He was thirty-three and I was eighteen; he took control of every aspect of my life. He hoped to shape me into his desired partner.

In the beginning, we were both in school, but that soon changed since we could not live on the meager salaries earned working part-time. I had to support us both while he finished school and got his degree. I worked around the clock, held three jobs, and had almost no time to sleep.

Emery was a complete control freak when it came to making decisions. He enjoyed arguing, and had a very eloquent way of expressing himself because of all the reading he had done. The law career suited him well. I hardly saw him, for he worked and studied at the school library. I went to work, kept house, and occasionally slept.

Soon I found out I was expecting, but kept working through the eight month. When our baby girl was born, Emery was overwhelmed! He had graduated from Loyola Law School, and was preparing to pass the Illinois bar. He named our daughter Charmaine, which he found exotic and unique. He had difficulty expressing his joy, so he talked baby talk and made silly faces to amuse her. Charmaine, my little Cookie, could do no wrong, and he indulged her as much as he could. At this time, he worked for a CPA firm, spending long hours downtown. Then I was expecting our second child, a son, Rod. He was a big boy at birth, weighing over nine pounds. I was overjoyed with the perfect family! Rod was quick and smart and grew fast, trying out everything his sister did, who was older. He was the cutest little boy, with his curly hair and big brown eyes. All we needed now was a dog, and we got one Rod picked out from the shelter, a black lab named Lucky.

Emery was about five feet eleven inches tall, average weight, and always meticulously dressed. Every detail was noticed: he had perfectly smoothly shaven cheeks, initials on his shirts, little silver cufflinks, and the perfect tie to go with every shirt. He was extremely detail oriented. His only physical activity was tennis, and he played with a pro from the club. Unfortunately, he and our son, Rod, never got along. Rod saw his shortcomings clearly, and pointed them out by making fun of them. This infuriated his father.

Emery was devoted to his job and providing for our needs. He worked long hours, spent little time with the kids, and wanted to buy a home and move to the suburbs. Once we moved out of the city, his commute became longer, and we saw even less of him. We all enjoyed living in Lake Bluff, a very isolated suburb. Emery was infrequently a presence, so we slowly drifted apart. I wanted a divorce, and finally got it.

Emery's parents were very much like him: cold and expressionless. He made the effort of trying to be a good father but remained cold, distant, and controlling. His life had been difficult, and he never learned how to be happy and loving. However, he gave me two wonderful children, and now, grandchildren. May he rest in peace.

Being a Yoga Teacher

≈

Once we moved to Sarasota, I began looking for yoga studios. I soon found Body and Soul in Towles Court, where I started taking lessons from Jaye Martin and Steven Weiss. Jaye told me about a studio called Garden of the Heart (GOH), which was newly started by Betsy Downing, a brilliant teacher. As soon as I met Betsy, I knew I had found my studio. It became "my home, away from home"; I spent so much time there. I signed up for the teacher training, which was a three-year program, to deepen my knowledge of yogic philosophy and become a better teacher.

At that time, GOH studio was teaching Anusara Yoga, whose founder was John Friend. When I first met John, I just fell in love with him, his energy, his loving presence, and his teaching style. We traveled to several of his workshops in Miami and as far away as Estes Park, Colorado for a workshop organized by *Yoga Journal*, which attracted over eight thousand of John Friend's followers. He called it the "Gathering." It was amazing to practice with the likes of Rodney Yee and other luminaries of the yoga community from all over the country. It was wonderful to have a chance to compare various styles and practices and to learn and develop one's own style.

A neighbor invited me to a class at the Woman's Resource Center, where I met Babe Wyler, who was in her nineties. She asked me to sub for her when she was traveling. I became a volunteer yoga teacher there and remained there, teaching twice a week until the center closed during the pandemic. I also volunteered at the Friendship Center and continued teaching at the GOH center until it closed during the pandemic. Betsy sold GOH studio to Cheryl and Tim Chaffy, and they moved it to a different location, much closer for me. Cheryl kept it open through April 2020, when we started teaching on Zoom from home, very conveniently.

At the beginning of 2022, I felt "all Zoomed out," missing the personal contact with my students. At this point, Harmony, a fellow yoga teacher, asked me to co-teach with her in person at Prana Yoga, a lovely studio owned by Regina Dewitt, who was also a friend from GOH. There I could take all the classes I wanted in exchange for teaching.

Through my yoga teaching, I met so many amazing teachers and made so many friends, and we always supported each other. Just to name a few: Cheryl, Gillian, Harriett, Harmony, Tama, Lill, Amanda, Jaye, and Randall. I went on yoga retreats with Jaye to Costa Rica, with Randall Buskirk to Bali, and with Nancy to Morocco. Yoga has been a very important part of my life, and continues to be my "health insurance" in more ways than one.

I feel blessed to have been introduced to yoga so early in my life by Uncle Phano. I also learned so much from Mother, who was a follower of Dr. Paul Brunton, the author of books on yogic philosophy. Dr. Brunton wrote about his travels in India and his guru. Some of his best-known titles are *The Secret Path, The Wisdom of the Overself,* and *A Search in Secret India*. Mother believed in the principles he had written about, and lived them daily, as did her Uncle Phano, Aunt Mila's husband.

Yoga has been a true blessing in my life!

Gallery

A collage with mother and daughters 1946

Aunt Mila in her car 1935

Father Eugene Molnar 1939

Father Eugene with his Mother

Father Eugene with sister Elsa 1928

Molnar family with employees 1942

Mother, father, Beck grandparents with baby Edith

Mother's family Beck

Pensionnat Notre Dame de Sion Buda Sashegy   Façade vers le jardin

Printed in the United States
by Baker & Taylor Publisher Services